THREE PLAYS ABOUT
IBSEN AND STRINDBERG

Michael Meyer

LUNATIC AND LOVER
A MEETING IN ROME
THE SUMMER IN GOSSENSASS

OBERON BOOKS
LONDON

Lunatic and Lover first published by Methuen Publishing Ltd.

This anthology first published in 2000 by Oberon Books Ltd.
(incorporating Absolute Classics)
521 Caledonian Road, London N7 9RH
Tel: 020 7607 3637 / Fax: 020 7607 3629

e-mail: oberon.books@btinternet.com

A catalogue record for this book is available from the British Library.

ISBN: 1 84002 193 4

Cover design: Andrzej Klimowski

Cover typography: Jeff Willis

Printed in Great Britain by Antony Rowe Ltd, Reading.

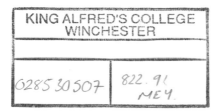

Contents

Introduction, 7

LUNATIC AND LOVER, 11

A MEETING IN ROME, 59

THE SUMMER IN GOSSENSASS, 89

INTRODUCTION

Michael Meyer

L *unatic and Lover* lasts 75 minutes and should, like the other two plays in this volume, be played without an interval. In it, I have tried to present a man of multitudinous contradictions whose life patterns repeated themselves in, as it seemed to him, a sick and nightmare way: the same female tormentors, the same male-establishment tormentors, the same periods of total isolation leading closer and closer to madness until at last he reached the brink and, unlike Van Gogh and Nietzsche, survived.

The conventional method of presenting a historical figure on stage is to start at an advanced moment in his life and look back. Although this works effectively with men of action, I do not think it has ever been successful with a creative artist, least of all one whose life story is unfamiliar to the average spectator, as is the case with Strindberg outside Sweden. I felt that the best way of realizing this in a theatre, especially the fringe theatre that commissioned the stage version of what started life as a radio play, was to attempt a method something like that of television documentary – many short scenes, some lasting only a few seconds, with, since I wished to avoid a narrator, the characters often speaking their own thoughts, as well as their letters and the letters they receive. It so happens that this is very much the method which Stindberg himself used in *A Dream Play*, which seemed an extra reason for employing it here. The effect, as in that play, was intended to be kaleidoscopic. If these 'multitudinous contradictions' of a tormented spirit sometimes produced the impression of a maelstrom, that seemed no bad thing; life to Strindberg was not something logical and consistent.

I have followed closely the known facts of Strindberg's life, as far as one can ascertain them; Strindberg was a compulsive liar, and many of his statements in his letters and autobiographical writings have been found to be untrue. My principal sources are, nevertheless, these letters and autobiographies, and of course his plays, which contain much autobiography, straight or distorted; a critic once remarked that Strindberg's work consists of fiction which is largely autobiography and autobiography which is largely fiction. I have drawn upon Frida Strindberg's *Marriage with Genius*, Harriet Bosse's comments on Strindberg's *From an Occult Diary*, which deals with his third marriage; and the many memoirs of him by his friends and enemies.

Andy Jordan's productions of *Lunatic and Lover* in Edinburgh in 1978, London in 1981 and New York in 1988 used Munch's paintings as the visual inspiration for the setting and, often, the groupings. The set comprised a circular rake painted with a reproduction of Munch's 'The Scream' and, in London, a cyclorama painted in wavy lines of dark blue and black. To the right and left of the stage, in full view of the audience, were two dressing areas where the actors and actresses, other than Strindberg, were seated as the audience entered and where, as the play proceeded, they altered their dress, hairstyle and make-up to take their different parts, watching that action when not thus engaged. The only furniture was a desk with a stool upstage centre and, for the first scene in the Black Porker Inn, the two stools downstage for Dagny and Munch as he sketches her. I have indicated the music cues used in these productions, though any future directors of the play are free to choose their own. I would earnestly beg that they eschew blackouts except where indicated on pages 17, 50 and 58.

I must thank the BBC for commissioning the radio and TV productions from which these stage versions grew, and most of all Andy Jordan for more suggestions than I can enumerate concerning re-shaping and re-writing, and for directing in all three cities with the kind of skill, imagination and intensity which Strindberg, in his lifetime, was seldom lucky enough to enjoy in the staging of his plays. Likewise, I owe a considerable debt to Casper Wrede and Richard Osborne for their many suggestions concerning *The Summer in Gossensass* and *A Meeting in Rome*.

A Meeting in Rome records a conversation that did not take place. Ibsen and Strindberg never met, though Strindberg, at the age of 35, then still an admirer of Ibsen for his iconoclasm and challenge to the social and moral order, planned to visit him in Rome in the spring of 1884. By the end of that year the seams of Strindberg's marriage had began to come apart, leading him into an irrational (if qualified) distrust of women, for whose baleful influence he now blamed Ibsen as the author of *A Doll's House.* But that spring their enthusiasms and contrasting opinions would have been almost equally shared, an area that has been surprisingly little explored. This play attempts to show how much they, and their wives, had in common as well as their differences.

The Summer in Gossensass tells of Ibsen's reciprocated infatuation at the age of 61 with an 18 year old Viennese girl, Emilie Bardach, and of its effect on his subsequent five deeply sombre plays, notably *Hedda Gabler* and *The Master Builder.* Ibsen told a friend how a young girl had tried to 'entrap' him, and when after his death his letters to her were published she was generally taken to be the original of those two memorable monsters, Hedda and Hilde Wangel in *The Master Builder.* Her subsequently discovered diary gives the lie to this, and Norwegian psychiatrist, Dr Arne Duve, has persuasively argued that Hedda is in fact a self-portrait of Ibsen in skirts, imbued with all his fear of scandal and longing for sex and fear of it. Likewise, in *The Master Builder,* Ibsen seems to have twisted Emilie's true character so as to make her rather than him seem the prime mover, much to Emilie's distress when she read it. *The Summer in Gossensass* seeks to explore that relationship and its consequences.

Michael Meyer
London, June 2000

LUNATIC AND LOVER

Characters

AUGUST STRINDBERG

SIRI VON ESSEN

FRIDA UHL

HARRIET BOSSE

STRINDBERG's FATHER

STRINDBERG's MOTHER

STRINDBERG's STEPMOTHER

THEATRE DIRECTOR

ACTRESS

ACTOR

BARON VON WRANGEL

ALBERT BONNIER

PROSECUTOR

MARIE DAVID

A MESSENGER

FIRST THEATRE CRITIC

SECOND THEATRE CRITIC

EDVARD MUNCH

DAGNY JUELL

STANISLAW PRZYBYSZEWSKI
(Shibishevski)

GIRL
(Wrangel's fiancée)

Lunatic and Lover was originally commissioned as a radio play by the BBC and was first broadcast in that version on Radio 3 on 19 April 1977, with the following cast:

AUGUST STRINDBERG, Alan Badel

SIRI VON ESSEN, Jocelyn Sbath

FRIDA UHL, Sian Phillips

HARRIET BOSSE, Caroline John

MARIE DAVID, Jane Knowles

ALBERT BONNIER, Jeffrey Segal

STANISLAW PRZYBYSZEWSKI, Peter Craze

BARON VON WRANGEL, Walter Hall

AUGUST FALCK, Peter Dennis

ANNA STRINDBERG, Joan Matheson

THE ADVERSARY, John Richmond

Director, John Theocharis

A stage version was commissioned by the Bristol Express Theatre Company, and was first performed by them at the Heriot-Watt Theatre, Edinburgh, on 19 August 1978, with the following cast:

AUGUST STRINDBERG, John Christopher Wood

SIRI VON ESSEN/STRINDBERG's MOTHER,
    Laura Davenport

FRIDAUHL/STRINDBERG's STEPMOTHER/
    MARIE DAVID, Adele Griffiths

HARRIET BOSSE/DAGNY JUELL, Jenny Seagrove

STRINDBERG's FATHER/ALBERT BONNIER/
    A POLICEMAN/STANISLAW PRZYBYSZEWSKI,
    Ian Ormsby Knox

THEATRE DIRECTOR/BARON VON WRANGEL/
PROSECUTOR/CRITIC/EDVARD MUNCH,
Jim Smith

Director, Andy Jordan

Designer, Jane Jet Harris

Lighting, Richard Moffatt

This version was much revised and, as here printed, was
performed by the Bristol Express Theatre Company at the
Old Red Lion Theatre Club, Islington, on 15 April 1981, with
the following cast:

AUGUST STRINDBERG, Miles Anderson

SIRI VON ESSEN/STRINDBERG'S MOTHER,
Lesley Duff

FRIDA UHL/ACTRESS/MARIE DAVID, Debbie Sack

HARRIET BOSSE/STRINDBERG's STEPMOTHER/
MESSENGER/DAGNY JUELL/A GIRL
(Wrangel's fiancée), Anna Lindup

STRINDBERG's FATHER/ACTOR/ALBERT
BONNIER/SECOND THEATRE CRITIC/
STANISLAW PRZYBYSZEWSKI, Jonathan Kydd

THEATRE DIRECTOR/BARON VON WRANGEL/
PROSECUTOR/FIRST THEATRE CRITIC/
EDVARD MUNCH, Nigel Hughes

Director, Andy Jordan

Designer, Louise Belson

Lighting, John Schwiller

On 26 May 1981 this production transferred to Theatrespace,
Covent Garden. The cast was unchanged.

The action takes place in various parts of Europe during the years 1853–1912

As the audience take their seats: Schoenberg's 'Variations for Orchestra'. Blackout. As STRINDBERG enters: Mahler's 'Symphony No. 9'. Lights up to reveal STRINDBERG surrounded by his three young wives, SIRI, FRIDA and HARRIET.

STRINDBERG: My life seems to have been ruled by two powers. One gives me everything I want while the other stands there and smears every gift with filth.

SIRI: You exaggerate.

STRINDBERG: Exaggerate?

FRIDA: (*To SIRI.*) He always exaggerated.

SIRI: Or lied.

STRINDBERG: Never consciously.

HARRIET: What difference does that make? You don't distinguish between reality and fantasy.

STRINDBERG: There's a deeper reality than what just happens.

FRIDA: But you agree you're an unreliable witness?

STRINDBERG: Only in details.

SIRI: Details matter.

STRINDBERG: I sought a larger truth.

HARRIET: Did you ever find it?

STRINDBERG: Sometimes I thought I caught a glimpse. At any rate, I did not mistake the mask for the real. Why do you mock me?

SIRI: Oh, dear. Here we go.

STRINDBERG: You mock me! All of you. What do you know of me? What can you know?

FRIDA/SIRI/HARRIET: We married you.

STRINDBERG: I loved you all. And you used me. All of you.
(*They start to leave him.*)
Whores, bitches, bloodsuckers!
(*They are gone.*)
I was mocked from birth.
(*The FATHER has entered behind STRINDBERG.*)

FATHER: August!

STRINDBERG: (*A small, frightened boy now.*) Yes, father?

FATHER: I thought I told you to stay in your room.

STRINDBERG: I was watching the men take the furniture. Why are they doing that, Father?

FATHER: That's no concern of yours. Now go up to your room and do your homework.

STRINDBERG: I've done it.

FATHER: Then recite your two times table.

STRINDBERG: (*Terrified.*) Yes, Father. One times two is two. Two times two is er – two, two.

(*He starts to work it out on his fingers. The MOTHER enters carrying boots.*)

MOTHER: I've polished your boots, Carl Oscar.

FATHER: Quiet! You were saying, August. Two times two.

STRINDBERG: Er – I know it, Father. I just can't say it.

(*The FATHER comes over and pulls his hair, keeping it pulled.*)

STRINDBERG: (*In pain.*) Ah!

MOTHER: Carl Oscar. You frighten the boy.

FATHER: And you spoil him. Now repeat after me. Two times two is four.

STRINDBERG: (*Still in pain.*) Two times two is four –

FATHER: Again.

STRINDBERG: Two times two is four –

FATHER: Again!

STRINDBERG: Two times two is four –

FATHER: (*Leaves go of his hair.*) Now go up to your room and repeat it to yourself one hundred times.

STRINDBERG: Yes, Father.

(*STRINDBERG withdraws, muttering: 'Two times two...' He stops and watches his parents as though in hiding. The FATHER has snatched the boots from the MOTHER and is examining them.*)

MOTHER: It's not his fault you've gone bankrupt.

FATHER: He needs it. He's lazy. And in future wear gloves when you polish my boots. (*He holds them up.*) They're scratched. You're not a chambermaid any longer, you know.

(*He goes. STRINDBERG lets himself be seen by the MOTHER.*)

STRINDBERG: Why do you let him talk to you like that?

MOTHER: You've been listening.

STRINDBERG: What does bankrupt mean?

MOTHER: August, you heard your father. Now go to your room.

STRINDBERG: It means he's dying, doesn't it?

MOTHER: No, it doesn't. He has great troubles.

STRINDBERG: I knew he was. I worked it all out. He's much older than you, that means he'll die before you –

MOTHER: August, please –

STRINDBERG: Oh, mother, won't it be wonderful! When he's dead, there'll be just us.

(*The MOTHER removes his arms from round her waist, lowers a black veil and goes.*)

Where are you going?

(*The FATHER enters.*)

FATHER: August, I have some good news for you. I am getting married again. And you know what that means, don't you? It means you will have a new mother, my boy.

STRINDBERG: (*Aged thirteen.*) I don't want a new mother.

FATHER: Now, now, August. You'll soon get used to it.

STRINDBERG: Least of all another of your servants.

FATHER: What do you mean?

STRINDBERG: That's who it is. It's the new housekeeper. Isn't it?

FATHER: How dare you? How dare you criticise my choice?

(*The STEPMOTHER joins them.*)

Kiss your new mother, August.

(*STRINDBERG and the STEPMOTHER kiss formally. She boxes his ear. The FATHER and STEPMOTHER leave, a happy couple. Church music.*)

STRINDBERG: (*Kneels downstage.*) Dear Father in Heaven. I am full of confusion; thou huntest me as a fierce lion; thou renewest my witnesses against me. Wherefore hast thou brought me forth out of the womb – ?

(*The FATHER enters.*)

FATHER: August.

STRINDBERG: Yes, Father?

FATHER: Your mother has suggested we go to the country for a picnic. Your brothers and sisters are getting ready. Why don't you do the same?

STRINDBERG: Today is Sunday, Father.

FATHER: That is precisely why we are going.

STRINDBERG: It is a sin to enjoy oneself on Sunday.

FATHER: A sin? Good God –

(*The STEPMOTHER enters, furious. She clutches a soup ladle, stained a bluey-green colour.*)

STEPMOTHER: Look at this ladle! The last time I looked it was solid silver.

(*STRINDBERG looks guilty. The FATHER snatches the ladle.*)

STRINDBERG: It's all right. It's still silver. It's just been dipped in a copper solution. I can get it off. I think.

FATHER: The choice is yours, August. Either those chemicals leave the house or you do. Do I make myself clear?

STRINDBERG: Yes, Father.

(*The FATHER hands the ladle back to the STEPMOTHER.*)

(*Aged eighteen.*) I have won a scholarship.

FATHER: A scholarship?

STRINDBERG: To Upsala. University! You don't seem very pleased.

FATHER: Of course I'm pleased for you. You're eighteen now, old enough to look after yourself. What do you want me to do? A jig?

STRINDBERG: I just thought –

FATHER: What did you think?

STRINDBERG: I thought you might offer to give me an allowance.

FATHER: Nonsense, I can't afford it.

STRINDBERG: Of course you can. You've paid off your creditors. You're earning more than a University professor now.

FATHER: Don't you tell me what I can and can't afford. When I was your age I'd already been earning for three years. Get a job and study at night.

STRINDBERG: You can't study medicine just at night.
I'll have to attend lectures and classes.

FATHER: Then get a night job. I managed on four hours
sleep when I was your age. You can do the same.

STRINDBERG: But –

FATHER: Argue all you want, lad, you'll get nothing from
me. It's time you grew up. And learned to face reality. (*He
goes.*)

(*Guitar music – a Swedish student song.*)

STRINDBERG: My dear brother. Here I am at last in
Upsala. I arrived with no more than a shilling in
my pocket. I wandered around with my books and
sleeping-bag and finally borrowed money for a room. It
is a mousehole with a camp bed, no more – no sheets or
pillowcases, not even a candlestick, nothing. I lie in bed
in my underclothes and read, with a candle in a bottle.
Luckily a chimney-pipe passes through the room, which
keeps me warm. Now and then friends bring me food.
(*He starts to read a slim book.*)
Father! Oh, this is wonderful! He attacks everyone,
everything. He says politicians are bugs. And the
Church, he says that's all humbug too and hasn't
anything to do with what Christ really taught. And
parents! (*Roars with laughter.*) He's got something to say
about them too. Oh, what a book! And he's written it as
a play! Fancy, using the theatre to spread ideas like
these! Who'll dare to put it on, though? (*He looks at the
book.*) *Brand* Henrik – Ibsen? Oh, if I could write like
that! (*He drops to his knees. Gloomily.*) My dear brother,
I have failed my preliminary examination. How I am to
face up to another year of these boring studies, I do not
know. But what else can I do?

DIRECTOR: (*Enters.*) You have some training as an actor,
Herr Strindberg?

STRINDBERG: No. But I have studied Goethe's treatise
on the art of acting. I have practised gymnastics and
fencing, walked as he directs, head erect and chest
expanded, arms swinging and fingers lightly closed. I go
into the woods to declaim and so strengthen my voice –

DIRECTOR: Have you ever seen actors at work?

STRINDBERG: Certainly. I have witnessed rehearsals, and read many plays.

DIRECTOR: Which plays impressed you most?

STRINDBERG: *Julius Caesar.* And Ibsen's *Brand.*

DIRECTOR: (*Coldly.*) You admire *Brand?*

STRINDBERG: (*Fervently.*) Yes! Ibsen is a Savonarola! A prophet!

DIRECTOR: But it is hardly a play anyone could *act.*

STRINDBERG: (*Protests.*) Oh, I –

DIRECTOR: However, you have a good appearance and an educated voice. I may be able to fit you in. I am staging Björnson's new play next month, *Mary Stuart in Scotland.* You know it?

STRINDBERG: Oh, yes! I am sure I could play John Knox. I exactly understand that kind of zealot –

DIRECTOR: How old are you, Herr Strindberg?

STRINDBERG: Nineteen. But... Or Darnley. I see Darnley as a Hamlet figure –

DIRECTOR: Young man, these are leading roles, and you have never yet set foot on a stage.

STRINDBERG: (*Sheepishly.*) Yes, of course.

DIRECTOR: Yes, well. (*He hands a script to STRINDBERG.*) Fourth nobleman.

(*Enter ACTOR and ACTRESS as Bothwell and Mary Queen of Scots. This scene played very melodramatically, except by STRINDBERG, who watches appalled.*)

ACTRESS: Ah, Bothwell, Bothwell!
I have loved you truly. Wouldst thou betray my trust?

ACTOR: Most noble Lady,
Betray thy trust?
These eyes have never looked
On other women lustfully.

ACTRESS: Thou knowest
I do not speak of lust, but of ambition.
Thou plottest with the lairds of rife and Orkney –

ACTOR: Untrue, untrue! I swear it by this cross
If thou believ'st me not, let Bothwell die!

(*Enter STRINDBERG as Fourth Nobleman.*)

STRINDBERG: (*Naturalistically.*) The Danish lords have come with a challenge to the Lord Bothwell.

(*They look at him contemptuously.*)

ACTRESS: (*To ACTOR.*) They seek thy life. I prithee, see them not.

ACTOR: Shall Bothwell shirk a challenge?

ACTRESS: For my sake!

ACTOR: Never!

ACTRESS: My dearest lord, I prithee!

ACTOR: Nay! (*To STRINDBERG.*) Bid them appoint a time and choose their weapons.

(*STRINDBERG goes.*)

If I be a traitor, then 'twere best I die.

And if I die, I die for Scotland.

ACTRESS: Bothwell, die not but live for me.

ACTOR: My queen!

ACTRESS: My love!

(*They kiss. SIRI and HARRIET applaud.*)

STRINDBERG: (*Returning.*) Herr Director! I demand to be auditioned for a leading role!

DIRECTOR: On what grounds?

STRINDBERG: I may lack experience, but these others! They simply declaim their lines. No thought, no feeling. Goethe says –

DIRECTOR: Very well.

(*The DIRECTOR turns and faces upstage.*
STRINDBERG walks upstage, turns.)

STRINDBERG: (*In a high, squeaky voice.*) Friends, Romans, countrymen! Lend me your ears. I come to bury Caesar, not to praise him –

(*The DIRECTOR and the others break into uncontrollable laughter.*)

(*Defiantly.*) So. They do not want me. Well, they shall take me. If not as an actor, then as a playwright.

DIRECTOR: The Director of the Royal Theatre thanks Herr Strindberg for his comedy *A Nameday Gift* but, although he finds it not altogether without talent, regrets that he cannot recommend its acceptance –

STRINDBERG: Perhaps my talent is not for comedy?

DIRECTOR: The Director of the Royal Theatre thanks Herr Strindberg for his verse tragedy *Hermione,* but regrets –

STRINDBERG: Perhaps a one-act drama?

(*The DIRECTOR goes.*)

(*Alone.*) My dear brother, my position is desperate, to say the least. I teach for two hours a day, work in the library, translate cheap novels for serialisation – it leaves me no time to think or do anything else. To work all day to be able to eat, and then to eat so as to be able to work all the next day, is a dreadful circle. I am tired of everything. Nothing new, no new faces, I am empty – I have lost faith in myself, and in the providence which rules our lives. If there were a God, He would do more than He does. So, we are free; and must fight our battles alone.

(*Music: Chopin's 'Prelude in F, Op 28, No 23'.*
Enter SIRI, radiant.)

(*Unwillingly.*) A crowded street in Stockholm.

A burning summer's day.

A face beneath a blue veil –

You glanced and turned away

Into the shop's doorway.

Your skirt's silk rustle died.

Your small heel tapped to silence.

I followed you inside –

(*Pause.*)

You are a whore, a lesbian, an unprincipled nymphomaniac.

SIRI: That's not what you said to me at first.

STRINDBERG: (*Unwillingly.*) No. (*In wonder.*) What is your name?

SIRI: Siri von Wrangel. My husband and I admire your work.

STRINDBERG: You know it?

SIRI: We saw *In Rome.* And *The Outlaw.*

STRINDBERG: Terrible plays.

SIRI: We thought them vital and challenging. When will they stage *Master Olof* ?

STRINDBERG: (*Surprised.*) What do you know of that?

SIRI: We have read it. My husband says it is the finest play yet written in Sweden.

STRINDBERG: He is a man of taste. Is he a writer?

SIRI: No. A captain in the Guards. We should be honoured if you would call on us.

STRINDBERG: I should be honoured

SIRI: Tomorrow?

STRINDBERG: Tomorrow.

SIRI: Six o'clock. Here is my card. Till then. (*She goes.*)
(*He looks at her card, smiles, then notices something on it and his face changes. He turns violently away and buries his face in his hands as though to vomit. Then he straightens himself and nervously walks across the stage and rings an invisible bell. BARON VON WRANGEL appears before him.*)

WRANGEL: (*Coldly.*) Well?
(*Music: Chopin's 'Minute Waltz', with party chatter.*)

STRINDBERG: I – I –

WRANGEL: (*As before.*) Have we met?

STRINDBERG: (*Embarrassed.*) My name is Strindberg. I –

WRANGEL: (*Heartily.*) Ah, my dear chap! Come in, come in! My wife told me she met you.
(*Other GUESTS appear and stand around talking and drinking.*)
You know how immensely we admire your work. We are both ardent lovers of the theatre.

STRINDBERG: Thank you.

WRANGEL: (*Indicates SIRI, talking to GUESTS.*) My wife wanted to be an actress, you know.

STRINDBERG: I didn't know.

WRANGEL: Yes. Go and talk to her.
(*STRINDBERG moves over to SIRI. WRANGEL watches them like a voyeur.*)

SIRI: You came, then?

STRINDBERG: Yes. I almost didn't.

SIRI: Why?

STRINDBERG: (*Looking around.*) These rooms?

SIRI: Don't you like them?

25

STRINDBERG: Fate is strange. (*He smiles.*) This was my parents' apartment. I spent the most wretched years of my youth here – saw my mother die, and her place taken by a stepmother. As I stood before the gate just now, I was seized by a sudden sickness. I nearly turned and fled. When I rang the bell – (*He stops.*)

SIRI: Yes?

STRINDBERG: I couldn't avoid the thought that my father himself might open the door.

SIRI: But he didn't.

STRINDBERG: No. Only your husband. Why didn't you become an actress?

SIRI: My husband said it would not be proper.

STRINDBERG: Oh?

SIRI: For the wife of a baron.

STRINDBERG: But he loves the theatre –

SIRI: As a patron. Excuse me.

> (*Another GUEST engages her in silent conversation. WRANGEL comes over to STRINDBERG.*)

WRANGEL: (*Slightly drunk.*) Tell me, Herr Strindberg. Do you find my wife beautiful?

STRINDBERG: (*Embarrassed.*) Very beautiful.

WRANGEL: But, tell me. Do you find her beauty warm, or cold?

STRINDBERG: (*Surprised.*) Warm.

WRANGEL: Really?

STRINDBERG: But with a maidenly reserve, as is proper –

WRANGEL: Maidenly?

STRINDBERG: A married woman can seem maidenly –

WRANGEL: Quite, quite. Well, you must see more of each other.

STRINDBERG: (*Confused.*) I shall be honoured.

> (*WRANGEL walks over to other GUESTS. SIRI comes to STRINDBERG.*)

SIRI: You have been having a talk with my husband.

STRINDBERG: He has been most gracious to me.

SIRI: I am glad.

STRINDBERG: You sound surprised.

SIRI: No, most men find him so.

STRINDBERG: (*Hesitantly.*) He said we should see more of each other.

SIRI: You and he?

STRINDBERG: (*After a moment.*) You and I.

SIRI: Well?

STRINDBERG: When can I see you next?

SIRI: I have to leave tomorrow for Finland. My mother is ill there.

STRINDBERG: I'm sorry.

SIRI: I'll get in touch with you when I return.

STRINDBERG: Let's not meet here.

SIRI: Why not?

STRINDBERG: There are ghosts in this house. I lived here a hundred years ago.

SIRI: A hundred years?

STRINDBERG: That's how old I am.

SIRI: (*Gently.*) Can't we lay those ghosts?

(*WRANGEL wanders over to them. SIRI moves to the other GUESTS.*)

WRANGEL: Doing anything tomorrow, Strindberg?

STRINDBERG: Er – no.

WRANGEL: Siri's off to Finland. I'll be on my own. Care to join me?

STRINDBERG: I –

WRANGEL: Dinner. Just the two of us. At my club, I thought.

STRINDBERG: Thank you.

(*SIRI and the others go. Lighting change. STRINDBERG and WRANGEL sit.*)

WRANGEL: Seven! Seven of them together! Seven! When they turned the lights on, one of them turned out to be his wife's sister! (*He roars with laughter, a long drunken, rising laugh.*) Think if it had been his own sister! (*He laughs helplessly and slaps STRINDBERG on the back.*) I say, have you heard the latest definition of a hypocrite?

STRINDBERG: No.

WRANGEL: A man who comes out of a French brothel doing up his flies instead of wiping his moustache. (*He roars with laughter again.*) You don't find it funny?

STRINDBERG: No.

WRANGEL: You're like my wife. She didn't find it funny either. You'd suit her, you know. Would you like to make love to her?

STRINDBERG: I don't think of her in that way.

WRANGEL: How do you think of her? As a madonna?

STRINDBERG: (*After a moment.*) Yes.

WRANGEL: (*Laughs again.*) Siri a madonna! Well, in one sense.

STRINDBERG: One sense?

WRANGEL: She's frigid. Not interested in – (*Hiccoughs.*)

STRINDBERG: Not interested in sex?

WRANGEL: Not interested in men, anyway. It's got one advantage, mind. She isn't jealous. She knows about Sonja.

STRINDBERG: Sonja?

WRANGEL: (*Confidentially.*) Little usherette at the Royal Theatre.
(*He turns and faces downstage as STRINDBERG speaks his thoughts.*)

STRINDBERG: You revolt and repel me. How is it that I like you? It is impossible, but I do. Is it because I already know that I will cuckold you, although I tell myself that my love is pure? One is always drawn to the man one cuckolds, as the cuckold is to the man who betrays him. But would I betray you if she had not led me on?

SIRI: (*Has entered during his speech.*) Liar.
(*WRANGEL wanders off.*)

STRINDBERG: The world knows you did.

SIRI: Because you said so in print.

STRINDBERG: Did I force *you*?

SIRI: Force, force. We loved each other. I have your letters to prove it. (*She takes them out and reads.*) 'I wish I were a thunder-cloud that could embrace you and annihilate you; I wish I were the sun that I might draw you up like

dew! Our love cannot die because we have acquired
wings, we could never weary of each other because each
day we are new!'

STRINDBERG: (*Bitterly.*) Never weary of each other!

SIRI: (*Continues reading.*) 'Beloved creature, you think you
lack genius because you think genius means a sharp
mind. No! You have the fire, it is this dark flame which
disturbs and torments you. You shall become an actress –
I shall create a theatre for you, I shall act with you
and write for you – and love you. Fulfil your destiny,
become the greatest actress in the land!' Yes, you wrote
beautiful letters.

STRINDBERG: (*Gently.*) My love. (*He goes to her.*)

SIRI: (*Gently.*) Yes. (*Pause.*) Don't move away from me.

STRINDBERG: I am ashamed.

SIRI: For his sake?

STRINDBERG: Yes. He is my friend.

SIRI: You know he has his mistress.

STRINDBERG: She is not the wife of his friend.

SIRI: I will leave him and become your wife.

STRINDBERG: That would be the worst betrayal.

SIRI: What, then?

STRINDBERG: I must go away.

SIRI: No.

STRINDBERG: I have already booked my ticket. I leave
tomorrow.

SIRI: Tomorrow?

STRINDBERG: For Paris.

(*He comes downstage and reads her letter to him.*)
My dearest August. I have news for you, though I do
not know whether it will make you rejoice or grieve.
I am with child – our child, for I have not slept with
him for over three months. Now, if you wish it, he must
divorce me, and we can be man and wife. Come back to
me and watch him grow big until we two become three.
(*Suspiciously.*) Is it mine?

SIRI: I made my stage debut last week, as Camille. How
nervous I was, I cannot tell you, but you will know.

STRINDBERG: Is it mine?

SIRI: It seems I am a success.

STRINDBERG: Only because of the scandal. A baroness, on the stage!

SIRI: Next month I am to play Jane Eyre. Tell me you love me.

STRINDBERG: I came back and married you. A bad actress, and a whore.

SIRI: Our child died.

STRINDBERG: Our? (*Suddenly violent.*) I worshipped a madonna, and find myself cuckold to a painted actress. You flirt with all men, even with your maid. Any man, any woman!

SIRI: These are insane suspicions.

STRINDBERG: (*Gently.*) You are the sun, you are the earth and light.

SIRI: You abuse me one minute, worship me the next. You are two people.

STRINDBERG: And you? Yet we had wonderful days together. Wonderful days, and nights.
    (*The DIRECTOR walks across, throws some newspapers down by them, and goes off the other side.*
    STRINDBERG reads them.)
    Siri, my novel is a success! Listen to this. (*He reads from a newspaper.*) 'Herr Strindberg's novel *The Red Room* is a witty and brilliant account of life in the Bohemian artistic circle of Stockholm.'

SIRI: (*Reads another.*) 'Herr Strindberg, who is only thirty, has a brilliant future assured.'

STRINDBERG: 'A new Voltaire'! What about that? Siri, let's paste them up on the walls!

SIRI: August! Our new wallpaper!

STRINDBERG: Never mind. We're going to be rich now.
    (*He pastes a cutting up.*)

SIRI: August! You're mad!

STRINDBERG: Yes, I'm mad, mad, mad! (*He seizes her and kisses her. A long embrace. He picks up another newspaper.*)
    'Herr Strindberg's new satire, *The New State*, is cheap and

nasty.' (*Reads another.*) '*The New State* is not a book that should be found in the drawing-room of any respectable family.' (*He throws them down.*) Damned idiots!

SIRI: Well, you do attack pretty well everyone.

STRINDBERG: I must. Ooh, it's gone home to them, though, hasn't it? It's gone home! Damn the politicians! Bugger the Church! Fuck the Royal Family!

(*They shriek with laughter. He kisses her violently. She responds.*)

SIRI: We were happy then. In Switzerland with our three children.

STRINDBERG: Only because I didn't know about you and that woman.

SIRI: You drove me into her arms. With your jealousies and suspicions.

STRINDBERG: They turned out to be justified.

SIRI: Not then. But after the trial, you believed everyone was against you.

STRINDBERG: (*Paranoically.*) It was the women who were behind it.

SIRI: Well, it was a book against women.

STRINDBERG: Only the kind who prefer a career to marriage and motherhood.

SIRI: You'd proclaimed yourself a rebel, you'd attacked every institution there was. Were you surprised when they turned against you?

STRINDBERG: But the way they did it!

(*ALBERT BONNIER, a middle-aged Jew, enters.*)

Bonnier! How good to see you! (*He embraces him warmly.*) Sit down, sit down. Well, being my publisher hasn't exactly ruined you, has it? How many copies has *Getting Married* sold now?

BONNIER: Nearly four thousand.

STRINDBERG: Four thousand! Well, that's not bad for a book of short stories, is it? I've good news for you. I'm planning a second volume. (*Pause.*) Aren't you pleased?

BONNIER: Something rather awkward has happened.

STRINDBERG: Well?

BONNIER: I have been served with a summons for blasphemy.

STRINDBERG: (*Incredulously.*) Blasphemy!

BONNIER: Because of a sentence in your opening story which it is suggested casts scorn on the sacrament.

STRINDBERG: You're not serious. (*Pause.*) Who is behind this?

BONNIER: The Palace.

STRINDBERG: The Palace?

BONNIER: Queen Sophia, as I understand.

STRINDBERG: That old cow? But – it can't succeed, surely?

BONNIER: My position is somewhat delicate, in view of the fact that I am a Jew. As you know, there is a good deal of anti-Semitism in Sweden just now. I am advised that although a jury would almost certainly acquit an ordinary Swede on this charge, they might well find against me.

STRINDBERG: Bloody Sweden! Bloody, bloody Sweden! So, what do you intend to do? Can I help in any way? I suppose they can't touch me as long as I stay abroad?

BONNIER: No. (*He smiles.*) Blasphemy is not an extraditable offence. (*Pause.*) You could help me, but I hesitate to explain.

STRINDBERG: Tell me.

BONNIER: As I said, my advice is that no jury would find against an ordinary Swede on this charge. If you returned and stood trial with me, you would almost certainly be acquitted. And they could hardly acquit you and condemn me.

(*Pause.*)

STRINDBERG: You say I would 'almost certainly' be acquitted?

BONNIER: Yes.

STRINDBERG: But if I wasn't?

BONNIER: We would both go to prison.

STRINDBERG: How long?

BONNIER: A year. Perhaps two. Believe me, if my advice had been that you ran any real risk, I would not have asked this.

STRINDBERG: I am much hated in Sweden. A pamphlet appeared last year denouncing me as a corruptor of youth. A Swedish jury might feel that I deserved prison, whether this blasphemy charge was justified or not.

BONNIER: That is true.

SIRI: But if you don't go, Mr Bonnier will almost certainly go to prison.

STRINDBERG: (*To SIRI.*) I know what you're thinking. If I'm the rebel I claim to be, I should not be afraid of prison. That's what you're thinking, isn't it?

SIRI: Are you afraid of it? For a year, even two?

(*He is silent.*)

(*Gently.*) How can you call yourself a rebel and not face your accusers? If they send you to prison you will be a martyr. Nothing that you could write could so advance the cause of radicalism.

(*Long pause.*)

STRINDBERG: As you wish.

(*The noise of cheering crowds.*

STRINDBERG alone in a spotlight.)

STRINDBERG: Siri! Siri, when I arrived at Stockholm Station I was greeted by – (*Incredulously.*) – cheering crowds! They escorted me all the way to my hotel. Many of them were working men. They regard me as their champion because of my political writings. I had to address them from the balcony of my room. I have received three hundred letters and telegrams of support, to say nothing of deputations and ovations. I have been abused, whistled at, crowned with laurels. Flowers have been thrown at me; and excrement. Detectives follow me everywhere. People seem more frightened of me than I of them.

(*The PROSECUTOR appears behind him.*)

PROSECUTOR: Is your name August Strindberg?

STRINDBERG: Tomorrow the trial begins. How shall I stand up to cross-examination? Will speech fail me, will I appear a fool? If so, what will that do for the cause of radicalism? Siri, wish me luck!

PROSECUTOR: (*Repeats.*) Is your name Johan August Strindberg?

STRINDBERG: (*Turns and faces him.*) Yes.

PROSECUTOR: Were you born in this city of Stockholm on January 22nd, 1849?

STRINDBERG: I was.

PROSECUTOR: Do you admit that you have written plays depicting carnal lust?

STRINDBERG: (*Nervously.*) So did Shakespeare.

PROSECUTOR: Answer the question.

STRINDBERG: Yes, I have.

PROSECUTOR: Do you admit that you have incited the youth of Sweden to disobey their parents?

STRINDBERG: Yes. The young should disobey. It is only natural.

PROSECUTOR: Do you admit that you have attacked and abused the established Church?

STRINDBERG: Yes.

PROSECUTOR: Do you admit that you enjoyed carnal intercourse with your wife before marriage?

STRINDBERG: (*More and more nervous.*) Yes.

PROSECUTOR: And that you have suggested that such a course is advisable for all men and women contemplating marriage?

STRINDBERG: Yes.

PROSECUTOR: And that you are therefore a corrupting influence? Well?

STRINDBERG: (*Nervously.*) No, I deny that. (*Gathering courage.*) In every age, the young should question and attack their elders. They should challenge the accepted dogmas of the establishment, as represented by their parents, and their employers, and by politicians and the Church. To deny that is to deny the course of nature. (*Warming.*) If you condemn me for that, then you must condemn many of the great men of history, Socrates and Luther and Galileo and Darwin – and Christ! Send me to prison if you will, as you and your like sent so many of those. History will laugh at you, and not only history.

Every country in the civilised world will mock you. It is the ones like you who attempt to stifle comment who are the true corruptors of youth!

(*The PROSECUTOR goes.*)

Siri, I am acquitted! They did not dare to send me to prison.

SIRI: Not dare?

STRINDBERG: There would have been riots. (*He laughs.*)

SIRI: You won. You beat them all.

STRINDBERG: But I never realised until I stood there how hated I am.

SIRI: Do you feel no sense of triumph?

STRINDBERG: Only of persecution. One newspaper demanded that all my books should be burned. Another described me as Lucifer.

SIRI: You told me they cheered you in the streets.

STRINDBERG: A few among millions. (*He whispers confidentially.*) Siri – I am surrounded by enemies.

SIRI: You attacked them all and are surprised that they hate you?

STRINDBERG: Surprised at their venom.

SIRI: You can't bear being hit back. You are a coward. (*She goes.*)

STRINDBERG: A dreadful coward. But not in print. Ibsen is the same. We are Galileos, not Luthers.

(*Suddenly alone.*)

My dear Brandes – sometimes I fear I may go mad. If this should happen and if I should lack the courage to kill myself – or should fail – I beg that you will arrange for me to be secretly poisoned –

(*SIRI and MARIE DAVID enter, entwined.*)

What are you laughing at, Siri?

SIRI: We were talking about men.

STRINDBERG: Who is this new friend of yours?

SIRI: Marie David. (*Davidde.*)

MARIE: I believe you know my father.

STRINDBERG: David?

MARIE: Georg Brandes. (*Brandess.*)

STRINDBERG: Are you his daughter?

MARIE: He says not. But my mother says yes.

STRINDBERG: Why do you dress like a man?

MARIE: You preach freedom, don't you?

STRINDBERG: Not freedom from responsibility. A woman's task in life is to be a wife and a mother.

MARIE: (*Laughs.*) And you call yourself a radical! You exhort the young to rebel against their parents, their teachers, the government, the church. But women have got to go on being bloody handmaids.

STRINDBERG: You haven't read my preface to *Getting Married.*

MARIE: That book.

STRINDBERG: I demanded in print that every woman should have the vote. That she should keep her own name when she marries and not take her husband's. That she should have the same freedom as a man to run wild before marriage and choose her companion. That once married she should have a separate bedroom, giving her the right to own her own body. You damned feminists don't read what I write.

MARIE: You only want us to have jobs where we can't compete with men, so we can be full-time wives and mothers. What does that leave us?

STRINDBERG: How can a woman be a proper wife and mother if she spends all day away from home?

MARIE: How can she be a wife and mother if she doesn't fulfil herself as a human being? Haven't you read *A Doll's House?*

STRINDBERG: Ibsen is mad. He has gone mad.

MARIE: He is the liberator. He is a true radical. You only pretend to be one. You are just the kind of old-fashioned reactionary whom you pretend to despise. Why did you leave Sweden to live abroad?

STRINDBERG: I needed to get away.

MARIE: *You* needed! What about your wife? Did you think about her career? How can she act in countries where she can scarcely speak the language?

STRINDBERG: How can she be a wife and mother if she is out every evening until midnight?

MARIE: Ah, was that why you went abroad? You wanted her to give up the stage. Yes, you are just like Heliner in *A Doll's House*. (*Maliciously.*) They had three children too.

STRINDBERG: (*Furious.*) Are you encouraging Siri to do what that damned Nora did?

(*MARIE and SIRI roar with laughter.*

MARIE kisses SIRI, then drifts-off. Soft piano music: Satie's 'Sports et Divertissements'.)

(*To SIRI.*) How long is that woman to stay here?

SIRI: I enjoy her company.

STRINDBERG: I can see that. You hold hands and kiss. (*Pause.*) Is she your lover?

(*Pause.*)

SIRI: What if she were? Have you never been unfaithful to me?

STRINDBERG: Then you admit it?

SIRI: I admit nothing. Only the right to have a lover, like you.

STRINDBERG: Of either sex?

SIRI: You want all men to be free, and no women.

STRINDBERG: How many other lovers have you had since we married?

SIRI: For God's sake! (*Pleadingly.*) Think of our children.

STRINDBERG: Are they ours?

SIRI: Now you are mad.

STRINDBERG: Am I? You betrayed your first husband, didn't you? Why not me? That first child who died – the one for whom I married you. Was that mine? Or was it just a trick?

SIRI: Of course it was yours. And the others too.

STRINDBERG: I can never be sure. They are yours all right, we know that. But neither you nor I can be sure that they are mine.

SIRI: I really think you'd better see a doctor.

STRINDBERG: Yes, you'd like that, wouldn't you? So that you could have me certified and locked up. They're calling Tolstoy mad now, did you know that? And Nietzsche. Have you been intercepting my letters?

SIRI: Why on earth should I do that?

STRINDBERG: I keep writing to people and getting no answer.

SIRI: Not everyone replies to letters.

STRINDBERG: You have been opening and destroying them.

SIRI: If you think all this, why don't you divorce me?

STRINDBERG: Ah, you'd like that, so that you could set up house with this lesbian. And teach our children her charming ways. If you want to know I have tried to divorce you.

SIRI: Oh?

STRINDBERG: I sent a petition to Stockholm. But we can't get divorced because we are living abroad. And I can't go back to Sweden because they regard me as a pariah there.

SIRI: Then we must go on living together.

STRINDBERG: (*Cunningly.*) You would like me to leave you. But I know that if I do, you will have the right to keep our children and keep them from me. So, we must go on living together. But that woman must leave.

SIRI: I wish her to stay.

STRINDBERG: I say she shall leave.

SIRI: If she does leave, she will stay in this town, and I shall visit her as often as I please. And you will not be there to spy on us.

STRINDBERG: Scheming bitch! (*Alone suddenly.*) All the old irrational fears are returning to me. Fear of loneliness – fear of people – of dogs – of the dark. I have ceased to call her my wife. Yet, such are her wiles, we still live together, fuck together, I cannot call it love. Yet it is not mere lust that drives me to it, in some strange way we are welded. I hate her, yet I love her – love and hatred can co-exist. I know I shall find no peace till I cleanse her from my system. Work. I must work. I must write. (*He sits at the desk, dips his pen, writes. After some moments, tenderly.*) Siri!

SIRI: (*Sleepily, fondly.*) Yes?

STRINDBERG: Why do you torment me so?

SIRI: (*Tenderly, as to a child.*) Sleep, sleep.

(*Music: closing bars, Chopin's 'Nocturne in G major'.*)

STRINDBERG: (*Excitedly.*) My dear brother! I am living quite idyllically here in the country, alone in a house with (*Laughs.*) – six women! My wife and I sing student songs, play backgammon, drink beer and live like newlyweds. Really, we are very happy. I am writing a play – I have called it *The Father*. Don't let it depress you when you read it. It is a work of fiction – well, fiction blended with reality. People will think it misogynous, but all my misogyny is theoretical – I couldn't live without women.

(*SIRI roars with laughter.*)

Why are you laughing, Siri?

SIRI: This play of yours. Do you really think anyone will put it on?

STRINDBERG: It is a masterpiece. It will make our fortunes. You wait. (*Pause. Gloomily.*) Every theatre in Sweden has rejected it.

SIRI: How shall we pay our bills?

(*STRINDBERG looks hatefully at MARIE. She returns his glance.*)

STRINDBERG: I suppose I shall have to pawn things again. (*He looks at MARIE.*) Since I seem to be the general provider.

(*SIRI and MARIE laugh and murmur sensuously together.*)

Why cannot I stop loving you? Your witchcraft is unbelievable. And still this other woman haunts our house, shares our bed.

(*He clutches his head. Alone in a spotlight.*)

It seems to me as though I walk in my sleep, as though reality and imagination are one. I don't know if *The Father* is a fiction, or if my life has been; but I feel that, at a given moment, possibly soon, it will cease, and then I will shrivel up, either in madness and agony, or in suicide. Through much writing my life has become a shadow-play; it is as though I no longer walk the earth, but hover weightless in a space that is filled not with air but with darkness. If light enters this darkness, I shall fall, broken. In a dream which often recurs to me at night I feel that I am flying weightless, and I find this quite natural, as though all conception of right and wrong, true and false, had ceased to exist for me, so that everything that happens, however strange, seems inevitable. *(Pause.)* Next month *The Father* is to have its Swedish premiere.

FIRST CRITIC: Herr Strindberg's new play *The Father* can suitably be summed up in Hamlet's exclamation: 'O horrible! O horrible! Most horrible!' Any other comment seems superfluous.

SIRI: (*Tender, maternal, as he weeps.*) Ignore them. They are pygmies. You are a genius.

STRINDBERG: (*Like a child.*) You still believe that?

SIRI: Of course.

STRINDBERG: I love you so much. Why do we ever quarrel?

SIRI: (*Sadly.*) Why?

STRINDBERG: You make me so jealous.

SIRI: (*Gently.*) You drive me to it.

STRINDBERG: I need you.

SIRI: We need each other.

STRINDBERG: If only you had a career.

SIRI: You keep saying women shouldn't have careers.

STRINDBERG: I know. But you are an artist. You could be a great actress.

SIRI: But we always live abroad. How can I act in German, or French?

STRINDBERG: I must found my own theatre.

SIRI: We hardly have the money to pay our bills.

STRINDBERG: A large room with dressing space, that's all we need. Now, write this down. 'To the people of Scandinavia. Since I intend to open an experimental theatre on the lines of the Théâtre Libre in Paris, I hereby invite plays of whatever kind to be sent to me for reading.' (*Pause. Gloomily.*) None of these are any good. I shall have to write everything myself after all. (*Pause.*)

Take this letter. 'My dear Bonnier. I take the liberty of offering you the first naturalistic tragedy of the Swedish drama. This play, *Miss Julie,* will be remembered in history.'

BONNIER: 'My dear Strindberg. I fear *Miss Julie* is much too 'risky', much too 'naturalistic' for us. We dare not publish it, as likewise I fear you will find difficulty in getting it produced.'

STRINDBERG: Dare not! Typical Swedish, typical bloody Swedish! 'Difficulty in getting it produced.' Can't he read, I told him we've got our own theatre now. He'll see. Once we've got it on, publishers will go on their knees for it.

(*Enter a MESSENGER.*)

MESSENGER: Herr Strindberg?

STRINDBERG: Yes?

MESSENGER: You are the author of a play called *Miss Julie,* advertised to open at this theatre tomorrow?

STRINDBERG: (*Proudly.*) I am.

MESSENGER: Well, you'll have to make other arrangements. The censor has banned it.

STRINDBERG: Banned it?

MESSENGER: (*Hands him a letter.*) Read this. (*Goes.*)

STRINDBERG: (*Glances at it.*) Everyone is against me. Everyone persecutes me.

SECOND CRITIC: Herr Strindberg's play *Miss Julie* having been banned by the censor, the author was compelled to present it privately last night for a single performance at the Copenhagen University Students' Union, a depressing little room on the first floor of a building in Bath-house Street.

STRINDBERG: People say I have persecution mania. I am persecuted.

FIRST CRITIC: For some unexplained reason, the play lasts only ninety minutes.

STRINDBERG: Why take more? It was enough for the Greeks.

SECOND CRITIC: And is inconveniently performed without an interval –

STRINDBERG: The interval is the curse of serious theatre.

FIRST CRITIC: Much of the dialogue seems wandering and inconsequential –

STRINDBERG: That's the way people talk when they're emotionally excited.

SECOND CRITIC: The play is disturbingly and unnecessarily outspoken about certain things not usually mentioned in polite society –

STRINDBERG: You're damned right it is. Like people wanting each other when they hate each other.

FIRST CRITIC: The title role was played by the author's wife, whose performance appears to be precisely opposed to what the author intended. She is too cold, much too cold.

(*The CRITICS shake hands and go.*)

SIRI: I didn't see you in the audience.

STRINDBERG: I didn't watch it.

SIRI: Why not?

STRINDBERG: You know why not.

SIRI: What do you mean?

STRINDBERG: You are having an affair with that actor.

SIRI: (*Vehemently.*) I am not.

STRINDBERG: Why deny it?

SIRI: Because it is untrue. How many hundred times have we had this dialogue? You suspect me with everyone.

STRINDBERG: Life is a circle.

SIRI: For God's sake let us break it, then. Once and for all. And not try to patch things up yet again.

STRINDBERG: Very well.

(*SIRI goes. Soft piano music: Satie's 'Sports et Divertissements'.*) The comedy of my marriage is over, after thirteen years of ecstasy and misery. Siri has returned to that Danish lesbian – to think of *her* taking my place in my children's lives, I have given up writing plays, and devote myself wholly to science. Chemistry and astrology much interest me, and especially alchemy. I seek a method of making gold. If I succeed, I shall probably become a professor. Have you seen that Ibsen has been stealing my ideas and characters? His new play, *Hedda Gabler,* is a blatant crib of my *Miss Julie.* My seed has fallen into his brainpan and fertilised. Now he carries my seed and is my womb!

(*Pause. Closing bars, Chopin's 'Nocturne in C sharp minor'.*)

I cannot stay in Sweden, so near to Siri and the children, I cannot visit them and see that Danish woman-devil in my place at the table, in the nursery, in my bed. I am going abroad again – to Berlin.

(*The Black Porker Inn. EDVARD MUNCH is seated with a young girl, DAGNY JUELL. The piano-playing increases in volume. STRINDBERG stands watching MUNCH and DAGNY.*)

MUNCH: (*To DAGNY.*) The Pole's in good form tonight.

DAGNY: Stachu is always in good form.

MUNCH: It's strange. I don't like what he writes, I don't much like him. (*The piano music stops.*) But when I hear him play, then I begin to understand what other people mean by joy.

(*PRZYBYSZEWSKI enters.*)

PRZY: Ah! To create, to drink, to make love and have friends like you! This is how life should be. (*He looks around.*) What does the name Black Porker mean to the world today? Nothing. But posterity will say, 'Here in this tiny inn in a back street of Berlin, there once gathered writers and artists from small unfashionable countries, rejected in their own time, who sowed the seeds of a mighty future.' (*He sees STRINDBERG, goes over to him and kisses his hand.*)

Master!

STRINDBERG: What?

PRZY: You are the great master, August Strindberg?

STRINDBERG: Who are you?

PRZY: Ah, you do not know me. I am from Poland. You have many admirers there, among the young. None more than me.

STRINDBERG: What is your name?

PRZY: Przybyszewski. Stanislaw Przybyszewski. I have had plays performed myself, and poems published.

STRINDBERG: How did you know me?

PRZY: I have seen your photographs.

STRINDBERG: Who is that man?

PRZY: Edvard Munch!

STRINDBERG: (*Uninterested.*) Oh?

PRZY: The greatest living painter. But he is reviled and mocked. His fellow Norwegians call his paintings obscene daubs. The Germans invited him to exhibit here but the result was the same. They had to close after eight days. 'Demented visions – naturalistic excesses – depths of depravity and tastelessness.

STRINDBERG: (*Laughs bitterly.*) Exactly what they say about me.

MUNCH: Do they?

STRINDBERG: Didn't you know?

MUNCH: I'm afraid I haven't read anything by you.

DAGNY: And he doesn't read newspapers. You mustn't be offended.

STRINDBERG: I'm not. I avoid newspapers too. Scandinavian newspapers, anyway. And I haven't seen any of your paintings. To be honest, I never heard of you until now.

PRZY: (*Shocked.*) Never heard of Edvard Munch!
(*DAGNY roars with laughter, goes across to STRINDBERG and kisses him.*)

DAGNY: I like you for that.
(*She returns to MUNCH.*
STRINDBERG, shaken, stands still for a moment, then goes over and looks at the painting.)

STRINDBERG: Extraordinary. (*He stares at it.*) May I see more?
(*MUNCH is silent.*)

DAGNY: He doesn't like showing his paintings to strangers.

PRZY: He doesn't like showing them at all.

STRINDBERG: (*To MUNCH.*) You must show them to me.

DAGNY: He keeps them in his room at the hotel. He doesn't let anyone in there, except me.

PRZY: Not even me.

STRINDBERG: (*To MUNCH.*) I wish to see them. (*Pause.*)

MUNCH: (*Quietly.*) Very well.
(*The lighting changes. STRINDBERG and MUNCH in MUNCH's hotel room. STRINDBERG is looking at the paintings.*)

STRINDBERG: Yes. Yes! Hatred. Jealousy. Agony. That's what life is about. Not like those damned Frenchmen. (*MUNCH laughs and makes a dismissive gesture.*)
Manet – Monet – Degas –

MUNCH: (*Breaks his reserve at last.*) Picnics, pretty dancers, people bathing, knitting – Comfortable, untroubled bourgeois lives. They do not know what suffering is. Have you read Hamsun's novels?

STRINDBERG: Hamsun?

MUNCH: Knut Hamsun. There's a passage in one of his books. 'All that matters is the disorderly confusion of the senses – the world of fantasy within us – the whisperings of our blood, the prayers of our bones.'

STRINDBERG: Yes!
(*MUNCH shows him 'The Scream'.
STRINDBERG stares at it.*)

MUNCH: When I painted this, I was at breaking-point. Nature was screaming in my blood. (*Confidentially.*) Have you ever seen a screaming sky? I have. It was as though the sky had opened a thousand mouths and screamed colour down on to the world. The colour shrieked. People say no sky ever looked like that. It did to me.

STRINDBERG: And to me.

MUNCH: Monet and Renoir see happy, peaceful landscapes. They exist too. But not for me. Sometimes, of course; but they are an illusion, so I do not paint them. I paint at night, here in this room, what I saw during the day.

STRINDBERG: We are Ishmaels, compelled to wander and never find a home.

MUNCH: The terror of life has pursued me ever since I first began to think. Do you drink absinthe?

STRINDBERG: No.

MUNCH: You should. It brings hallucinations. Marvellous hallucinations. It frees the mind. One knows then that one's visions are the real truth. That there is a greater reality than what other men see.

STRINDBERG: A greater reality!

(*Suddenly they are back at the Black Porker inn. DAGNY slips off her dress and poses naked for MUNCH. He adjusts her hands on her lap, touches her head forward, so that she is as the girl in his painting 'Puberty'.*)

PRZY: (*Indicating DAGNY.*) She drinks more absinthe than anyone. Her capacity is amazing. She is our leader – the inspiration of us all.

STRINDBERG: Is she his mistress?

PRZY: His and mine. We have no bourgeois prejudices here. Our philosophy is that of Baudelaire and Verlaine. Love must be free. As you have preached.

STRINDBERG: I have never preached that.

PRZY: But you implied it.

MUNCH: (*To PRZY.*) Stachu!

(*PRZY goes over and MUNCH arranges him and DAGNY into the pose of his painting, 'Vampire', with PRZY's head in her lap and her bending over him as though sucking blood from the back of his neck.*)

Kneel down in front of her. Place your head against her.

STRINDBERG: That is not free love. Free love is love without the bond of marriage, but with commitment. Freedom without responsibility is anarchy. Degeneracy! And yet – how pure and virginal she looks! Two men. How could she?

MUNCH: (*To DAGNY and PRZY.*) Rest.

(*DAGNY breaks her pose, stretches, walks over to MUNCH and kisses him. STRINDBERG turns his back, jealous. DAGNY releases herself from MUNCH, walks across and kisses PRZY. STRINDBERG turns, compulsively watches them. PRZY whispers to her. She nods, goes over to STRINDBERG*)

and kisses him. DAGNY and STRINDBERG lie down together.
Lights down to near darkness.)

DAGNY: Why are you so shy in bed?

STRINDBERG: You think me shy?

DAGNY: This darkness. Lovers should see each other.

STRINDBERG: I regard love as sacred.

DAGNY: Why be ashamed of it, then?

STRINDBERG: I am not ashamed of it.

DAGNY: Don't be angry. You're a good lover. I thought
you hated women.

STRINDBERG: Only when they are not women. When they
try to usurp the place of men. And when they – (*He stops.*)

DAGNY: Yes?

STRINDBERG: Can you not be faithful to one man?

DAGNY: Why should I? Men aren't faithful to one woman.

STRINDBERG: I was.

DAGNY: More fool you. Stop talking now.

STRINDBERG: In the morning, one of her lovers paints
me. In the evening, I make love to her. And in the
afternoon, her third lover kisses my hands and calls me
master. (*Pause.*) She was a whore, but what a whore!
A few years later she was murdered by another lover.
My plays were performed in Berlin, and were a success!
First *The Father,* then *Miss Julie* and *Creditors.* And
Antoine staged *Miss Julie* in Paris. It was abused, but
acclaimed too. Then I met that other whore.

FRIDA: You idealised us till we slept with you, and then
you called us whores.

STRINDBERG: You were whores.

FRIDA: All of us?

STRINDBERG: All the ones I wanted. (*Bitterly.*) I was
drawn to that kind of woman.

FRIDA: I was never unfaithful to you while we were
married.

STRINDBERG: What on earth did I see in you?

FRIDA: I first met Strindberg in January 1893, at a party in
Berlin. I can see him now in the shadows – like a rugged
grey rock. So this is he, the lover of truth who unmasks

the lie. Who adores woman and lashes her for not being divine. He carries his head so high. His eyes are doors of eternity. I never imagined so much light could radiate from a human being.

STRINDBERG: What do you do, young lady?

FRIDA: I am a journalist.

STRINDBERG: Ah. You write about what?

FRIDA: I am a drama critic.

STRINDBERG: Ah.

FRIDA: I know your plays, of course. I was among the crowd that awaited you when you stepped off the train in Berlin.

STRINDBERG: Oh?

FRIDA: (*Young and eager.*) To us you are the Redeemer!

STRINDBERG: From what do you expect me to redeem you?

FRIDA: We seek the soul in things. To us you are the prophet. What does it feel like to be a prophet?

STRINDBERG: One pays.

FRIDA: How do you mean?

STRINDBERG: To be in advance of one's time is an expensive thing. I preach in the desert, and that in the end renders any voice shrill and hoarse. I do not think I shall write any more plays. I shall come myself to science.

FRIDA: Science?

STRINDBERG: In science one does not need an audience. One expects to be alone. (*Confidentially.*) I have discovered that sulphur is not, as has been supposed, an element. I shall unmask it and force it to reveal its complexities.

FRIDA: Oh?

STRINDBERG: Not only that. I have evidence that carbon, and nitrogen too, are likewise complex rather than elemental –

FRIDA: Next day, walking through the city, I felt unaccountably drawn to a certain spot, and there I saw him standing beneath a tree, drawing with his stick in the sand. I did not wish to disturb him, but suddenly, without raising his head –

STRINDBERG: So there you are.

FRIDA: You did call me, then? I felt it. Why are you standing here on the street corner?

STRINDBERG: I must stand somewhere while I wait.

FRIDA: What are you waiting for?

STRINDBERG: If only I knew. Happiness, or just the end of sorrow. If only I knew why I exist, why I stand here, where I must go, what I must do. Shall we take a walk?

FRIDA: Why not? (*Pause.*) Who is this August Strindberg with the shining eyes, the gentle mouth?

(*STRINDBERG laughs happily.*)

There are times when you can be as simple and gay as a child, when you laugh as a babe laughs. I dare say you could kiss too, and hold a woman in your arms. I ask myself how it would be to be kissed by you.

(*Pause.*)

STRINDBERG: Will you marry me, Frida?

FRIDA: Marry you?

STRINDBERG: You think I am too old? I am forty-four.

FRIDA: No. But – marriage! I will gladly go away with you – this very night. But I do not want to marry yet.

STRINDBERG: Marriage is a much misused institution, but it remains the best existing shelter for man, woman and child.

FRIDA: In matrimony we two will be stifled.

STRINDBERG: We shall never be stifled. We shall discover life anew every day.

FRIDA: (*Thinks aloud.*) My answer must be no. What kind of life would it be to be married to such a genius? I would have no thoughts of my own, no feelings of my own – no life of my own. I would lose myself, I must say no.

STRINDBERG: Well?

(*She looks at him fearfully. Long pause. They join hands.
WRANGEL enters with a GIRL on his arm.*)

WRANGEL: Strindberg!

STRINDBERG: Yes?

WRANGEL: (*Heartily.*) I read about your engagement. Splendid news! Congratulations!

STRINDBERG: (*Embarrassed.*) Thank you.

WRANGEL: Honeymoon?

STRINDBERG: England.

WRANGEL: I too am to remarry. This young lady has agreed to become my wife.

STRINDBERG: (*Formally.*) I congratulate you both.

WRANGEL: We must keep in touch. Here's my card. Don't forget! (*He goes off with the GIRL.*)

FRIDA: Who was that?

STRINDBERG: Baron von Wrangel. My first wife's first husband. Why should he wish me luck? I destroyed his marriage. (*Pause.*) Perhaps it was not a wish but a curse. Did I ever show you a photograph of Siri?

FRIDA: (*Unwillingly.*) No.

STRINDBERG: (*Takes out a photo.*) She's beautiful, isn't she? Aristocratic – refined – slender –
(*Blackout. Flashes of lightning. Sea sounds. FRIDA doubles up, retching.*)

FRIDA: Oh, God! I want to die.
(*More lightning. Suddenly they are seated quietly, he reading, she staring into space.*)
I hate this place. Can't we go on to London?

STRINDBERG: The Powers have told me that we must stay here.

FRIDA: What a name for the place to spend one's honeymoon! Gravesend!

STRINDBERG: You were too ill to be moved when we landed. Now the Powers wish us to stay.

FRIDA: The Powers!

STRINDBERG: Do not mock them.

FRIDA: I wish I'd died on that ship. August! This is our honeymoon. And we've spent a whole week of it in Gravesend.
(*They walk upstage, then turn.*)

STRINDBERG: Today we arrived in London. This is a good country. The gin is weak but the beer is strong. I don't see any of the famous chimney-smoke. A Dutchman named JT Grein, who runs an experimental theatre here, wants to stage a season of my plays, and has lent us his flat in – (*He hesitates.*) – Pimlico.

FRIDA: August! What a splendid apartment. You'll be able to work here. You'll be able to write.

(*STRINDBERG goes to the desk, opens a drawer. Out fly scripts and books. He picks them up, looks at them.*)

STRINDBERG: Frida.

FRIDA: Yes?

STRINDBERG: The Powers are against me.

FRIDA: What is it now?

STRINDBERG: Look at this. I open a drawer and out flies a mass of other men's plays.

FRIDA: It's Grein's flat and he runs a theatre. What do you expect?

STRINDBERG: Yes, but do you know whose plays these are?

FRIDA: No, whose are they?

STRINDBERG: Ibsen's. My arch-enemy.

(*FRIDA laughs.*)

Yes, you laugh, you're on his side. And – (*He looks at a script.*) – someone called Shaff.

FRIDA: Shaff? What's he? Russian?

STRINDBERG: I don't know.

FRIDA: (*Looks at script.*) Shaw.

STRINDBERG: Shaw. (*He glances at opening pages, tosses it on to the floor. Looks at it and the Ibsens defensively.*) Look at them. They lie crouched, ready to spring. Am I to sit quietly by while other men's plays are born and buried? Must I, the pioneer, write in a room where the battle for Ibsen is still in progress?

FRIDA: Oh, for God's sake! Where else do you suggest we stay? We can't afford a hotel.

STRINDBERG: What, then?

FRIDA: You must go back to Germany. I shall stay here.

STRINDBERG: If I leave you now, shall we ever meet again?

FRIDA: (*Uncertainly.*) Of course.

(*Pause.*)

He wandered restlessly across Europe. After some months I joined him in Berlin. One morning his coffee was not hot enough. He shut himself into his room. Then a long white sheet of paper came gliding in beneath my door, like an evil snake, with hateful and extraordinary things written on it –

STRINDBERG: You have deliberately been undermining my health by your bad cooking, by choosing the food you know will make me ill, by waking me at night, then turning from me. It is clear that you are tired of me and that you have a lover. Last night 1 smelt his sweat on your body. You are a poisoner and a whore, you have eaten me hollow, sucked me dry.

FRIDA: Again I left him. Again we reunited. (*To STRINDBERG.*) I am with child.
(*Pause.*)

STRINDBERG: Mine?

FRIDA: How can you ask that?

STRINDBERG: My first wife betrayed me. Why not my second? You had lovers before you met me.

FRIDA: Not since.

STRINDBERG: What do you want me to do? Take a job as a clerk? Or a labourer? (*He sits angrily.*)

FRIDA: For a while we were happy. Then his distrust began to return. He imagined hatred everywhere –

STRINDBERG: Your mother has been here, hasn't she?

FRIDA: No.

STRINDBERG: And you were talking about me. I can almost hear the echo of her voice. I can feel her words poison the air and see them darken the sunlight. I think I can even see the impress of her body in the air. She leaves a smell after her like a dead snake.

FRIDA: I promise you, no!

STRINDBERG: You are different from when I married you. You should not have read that book which I forbade you to open.

FRIDA: It was like eating of the Tree of Knowledge. I saw –

STRINDBERG: Yes?

FRIDA: (*Whispers.*) How evil you are. I once read a story by Gogol. A bachelor has a dream on the eve of his wedding.

He dreams that he is already married and sees his home and his wife in it. He sees her everywhere. He looks at the bed, there lies his wife. He goes to the table, there she sits. He opens the cupboard, his wife springs out of it into his arms. He draws out his handkerchief to wipe the sweat of fear from his brow – his wife slips from his pocket. I am this appallingly ubiquitous wife. (*Pause.*) It is not Siri you wrote about. It is me. Soon it will be my turn. You will imagine these things about me. And write them, in a book or a play. You believe what you imagine. You *are* mad.

STRINDBERG: You *have* eaten of the Tree of Knowledge.

(*He moves away.*)

FRIDA: Where will you go? Back to Sweden?

STRINDBERG: No. They are staging *The Father* in Paris. I once found a kind of happiness there. Or anyway, contentment.

FRIDA: Will you be able to write there?

STRINDBERG: I do not wish to write.

FRIDA: Sulphur again? And gold?

STRINDBERG: You speak as if they were illusions, and the theatre were not.

FRIDA: Goodbye.

(*Music: Chopin's 'Prelude in D minor, Op 28, No 24'.*)

STRINDBERG: Goodbye.

(*FRIDA goes.*)

In Paris, *The Father* was staged, and was acclaimed. (*An audience is heard cheering.*) But it only brought me three hundred francs. Again, the theatre repelled me. I found peace in six crucibles of fine porcelain, which I robbed myself to buy. In a miserable student's room in the Latin Quarter, I made my laboratory. In the stove I raised the fire to furnace heat, secured the door and drew down the blinds, lest I should be arrested as a plotting anarchist. By the time dawn rose, I had ascertained the presence of carbon in sulphur. But from my hands, roasted by the intense heat, the skin was peeling off in scales. I could scarcely undress myself.

Yet alone in bed I was blissful. I felt pure, masculine, virginal. I saw my married life – lives – as something unclean.

(*The music fades.*)

When I reflect upon my work, I can see that the hand of the Unknown was disciplining me, driving me on towards a goal I was still unable to discern. Once it had been revealed to me that an unseen hand was guiding my steps along this rough path, I no longer felt alone. I felt personally acquainted with this unknown power, who chastised in order to reform. I talked to Him, thanked Him, asked His advice. Sometimes I imagined Him to be my servant, like Socrates's daimon. He led me into a new world where none could follow me. I thought of myself as one dead, passing my life in another sphere. I conceived a hatred for my fellow men. Then came my fall. I realised that He – that the Powers were displeased with me. The hand of the Unseen was raised against me, and its blows rained thick and fast upon my head. A drunken man stared at me today, mockingly. Then a young man laid a penny on my table as though I was a beggar. I moved to another table and the waiter followed me and gave me the coin again. That Pole began to haunt me – Przybyszweski. He'd married his girl – our girl – and was jealous of my having been her lover. I knew he was in Paris because I kept hearing him playing his favourite piano piece, Schumann's *Aufschwung,* as only he could play it. Every afternoon between four and five for a whole month. They told me he was nowhere near Paris, not even in France. (*Cunningly.*) But I knew. He wanted to kill me, to take his revenge. But I was too clever for him. Then the stranger arrived. (*Conspiratorially.*) A man came to live in the room next to my writing desk. He never spoke. But I could hear him writing as I wrote. And every time I pushed my chair back, he did the same. He repeated all my movements, deliberately imitating me so as to annoy me. When I went to bed, he went to bed too, but (*Cunningly.*) – in the room on the other side, next to my bed. He was occupying both rooms. And at night, in the gloom (*With increasing terror.*) – I could feel someone watching me, someone who touched me tightly, groped for my heart, and sucked. Aah! (*He collapses in terror. Pause.*) Then a friend came to me from beyond the grave, and explained why we humans suffer these ordeals. My great compatriot Emmanuel Swedenborg. (*Confidentially again.*) He made me understand that we are punished for our sins by a just God. Not only for our sins. For mankind's. Hell does not lie ahead of us. We are already there. I was in Hell, and damnation lay heavy upon me. Swedenborg convinced me that there was a God, and I saw myself as Job, the righteous and blameless man, put to the test by the Eternal. I was one of the chosen. And so, I was able to challenge the demons.

(*He stands. Suddenly he is composed. Music: Fauré's 'Prelude in F major, No 4'.*)

November 15th, 1900. First dress rehearsal of *To Damascus*. *I* went on to the stage and thanked Harriet Bosse, the young Norwegian actress whom Falck had cast as the Lady. As we stood there on the stage surrounded by a lot of people, her little face changed, grew larger and became supernaturally beautiful, seemed to come closer to mine while her eyes enveloped me with their luminous blackness. Then, without excusing herself, she ran away and I stood amazed. After this she haunted me for three days so that I could feel her presence in my room. Then I dreamed about her. She was married to me. She gave me her foot to kiss. She had no breasts, absolutely none. Her mouth when she smiled was like that of an eight-year-old child –

HARRIET: Dear Herr Strindberg. Thank you for the photograph. You made me so happy by sending it.

STRINDBERG: I woke at two o'clock. Possessed her when she sought me.

HARRIET: I have read only part of *The Dance of Death*. I cannot bear to read much at a time, it affects me so deeply. May I please keep it a few days longer?

STRINDBERG: At four o'clock I was overcome by an attack of weeping – wept over my own misery and that of mankind, with a premonition of coming disaster. Woke in the morning determined to free myself from her... She came, lovely, childlike, gentle, wise.

HARRIET: He told me how severely and harshly life had treated him, how much he longed for a ray of light, a woman who could reconcile him with mankind and with woman. Then he laid his hands on my shoulders and asked –

STRINDBERG: Will you have a little child by me, Miss Bosse?

HARRIET: I curtsied and answered, quite hypnotised: 'Yes, thank you'. And then we were engaged.

STRINDBERG: May 6th, 1901. Married for the third time. (*They turn to the audience, like a photograph of a newly-married couple. They come downstage, then move apart.*)

HARRIET: Dear August. This time I have left you for ever. Do not try to contact me. (*Pause.*) I came back to him, left him, came back. Left. I could not live with him, yet I could not stay away from him. Even after our divorce, I met him constantly and we would live together man and wife. We loved each other, and hated each other. August!

STRINDBERG: (*Longing for her.*) Harriet!

HARRIET: August, we must never meet again.

STRINDBERG: We shall always meet.

HARRIET: August, I am engaged.

STRINDBERG: You are engaged to me.

HARRIET: I am engaged to another man. An actor.

STRINDBERG: You can never be anyone's wife but mine. The Powers have said so. They spoke to me last night, clearly.

HARRIET: August! You must live with reality.

STRINDBERG: What do you know of reality? What you call reality is simply the material world. There is a higher reality –

HARRIET: Hallucinations.

STRINDBERG: The material world is a hallucination.

HARRIET: (*Sits behind him, holding him gently.*) He frequently imagines that I have come to him when I am hundreds of miles away. Even though I have seen him for the last time, he still believes I am living with him –

STRINDBERG: Now she is to be another man's wife. Yet at night she flies to me. We live as if we were newly married. All evening she was with me. Three times during the night she woke me and I received her as my wife. The next afternoon, a scent of roses that threw me into ecstasy. Several times that day she sought me; but I resisted her. On Easter Saturday, shortly before midnight, she sought me, kindly, lovingly. I made love to her four times. She sought me like fire and roses, roses in my mouth.

HARRIET: You must stop writing to me and thinking about me. I belong to another man, next month I shall marry him. Only wish me happiness. I believe in happiness.

STRINDBERG: Happiness! Life is a punishment, a hell. (*He cries softly.*) Ah! Now – she is married. (*He sighs with relief.*) Towards morning I began to feel I was liberated from her. It was as if many small knotted strings were being untied in my trunk – first in the nerves of my spine, then in my spleen, my liver, my lungs, my heart, my stomach and the small of my back. I felt blessedly delivered; got up, washed my whole body, put on clean linen and went out. Now I am alone. (*He stands.*) My best plays remain unperformed. *Miss Julie* had to wait sixteen years before they would stage it in Sweden. *The Dance of Death* will have to wait nine years. A *Dream Play*, five years. Even the ones that are performed are greeted with incomprehension. In desperation I found my own theatre to stage them but it fails and goes bankrupt. Now I am sixty. I shall write no more plays.

(*Cheering is heard outside.*)

What is that noise?

(*Now the other ACTORS and ACTRESSES abandon their characters and speak as themselves.*)

FIRST ACTOR: (*Wrangel.*) It is your sixtieth birthday. A crowd has come to cheer you.

STRINDBERG: To cheer me?

SECOND ACTOR: (*Bonnier.*) Telegrams will arrive all day. Flowers, laurel wreaths, addresses of congratulation –

STRINDBERG: From whom? The critics mock me, the theatres reject my plays. From whom?

FIRST ACTRESS: (*Siri.*) From the young. They are the ones you have always championed. They have no public voice, no newspapers. But they are your disciples. The cheering is heard very loudly.

FIRST ACTOR: Doesn't that sound give you joy? These, not the men and women who mock you, are the ones who hold the future.

(*STRINDBERG laughing cynically. Then he gives a short gasp of pain.*)

SECOND ACTOR: Why do you groan?

STRINDBERG: A slight pain. It is nothing.

SECOND ACTRESS: (*Frida.*) It is cancer of the bowels. It will torment you for three years, then kill you.

STRINDBERG: That too.

THIRD ACTRESS: (*Harriet.*) Remember what you wrote? It is the chosen ones who suffer.

STRINDBERG: (*In agony, dying.*) Oh, God! After sixty years of agony, I beg that I may be permitted to depart this life. The little joy I found in it was illusory or false. My work was the only thing worthwhile, but that was largely wasted, or useless, or harmful. Wives, children, home, were all a mockery. Women gave me happiness, but it soon evaporated. And through it all, I suffered from being human. From feeling my sight weakened by eyes, my hearing muffled by ears, and my thought, my light, airy thought, cabined by the windings of a brain. Now at last I shake the dust from my feet – the earth, the clay. Once I sat in the sunlight, on a verandah, under the first green leaves of spring. Now I have nothing more to say. (*Music: Chopin's 'Prelude in D minor, Op 28, No 3'. Fade to blackout.*)

The End.

A MEETING IN ROME
a conversation for the theatre

Characters

HENRIK IBSEN
aged 56

AUGUST STRINDBERG
aged 35

SUZANNAH IBSEN
aged 48

SIRI VON ESSEN
aged 33

NARRATOR

A Meeting in Rome was commissioned by the BBC, and was first performed on Radio 3 on 29 October 1991, with the following cast:

HENRIK IBSEN, 56 David Suchet

AUGUST STRINDBERG, 35 Martin Shaw

SUZANNAH IBSEN, 48 Ann Mitchell

SIRI VON ESSEN, 33 Kate Buffery

NARRATOR, Michael Meyer

Director, Andy Jordan

Rewritten for the stage, it was first performed at the Old Red Lion Theatre, Islington, on 7 May 1993, with the following cast:

HENRIK IBSEN, Kenneth Haigh

AUGUST STRINDBERG, Andy McEwan

SUZANNAH IBSEN, Margaret Robertson

SIRI VON ESSEN, Joanna Myers

NARRATOR, Michael Meyer

Director, Richard Osborne

On 12 August 1994 it was performed at the Pleasance Theatre, Edinburgh as part of that year's Edinburgh Festival. The cast was unchanged, except that Suzannah Ibsen was played by Jill Graham and Henrik Ibsen by Brett Usher.

STRINDBERG: (*In spotlight, malevolently.*) Ibsen's spirit is sick and aging. He has nothing to teach me. He speaks only for women and the young, and is consequently hated by grown men. He is one of the worst humbugs of the age.

NARRATOR: (*At side.*) So Strindberg wrote in 1904 at the age of fifty-five, in his novel *Black Banners*. Most people think of him as having been a lifelong enemy of Ibsen. But he wasn't. For more than half of his life, Strindberg was a fan of Ibsen. In February 1884, just after his thirty-fifth birthday, he wrote from Switzerland, where he was then living, to two friends of Ibsen asking them to give him an introduction. Dear Bjoernson and Lie –

STRINDBERG: Surely I should visit Ibsen in Rome! Will you be so kind as to ask him to receive me, since if he shows me the door I shall feel hurt. I want to see the angriest man in Europe before I die!

(*IBSEN and SUZANNAH enter and sit.*)

NARRATOR: Ibsen was then coming up to fifty-six. He had been living abroad for twenty years, first in Italy, where after a string of failures in Norway he had written his first real successes, *Brand* and *Peer Gynt*. Then he spent twelve less productive years in Germany, completing a long historical epic, *Emperor and Galilean*, a political range-finder called *The League of Youth* about the kind of insincere socialist whom he, as a lifelong socialist, most despised, and another political play, *The Pillars of Society*. In 1880 he returned to Italy and, in the space of three years, wrote the three plays which were to make him world-famous, *A Doll's House*, *Ghosts* and *An Enemy of the People*. He was now planning a work which was to confuse and antagonise his disciples, though it is today regarded as one of his greatest. He wrote to his friend Georg Brandes –

IBSEN: I am struggling with the draft of a new play which will be somewhat different from my recent works. Unlike them, it won't deal with topical problems, such as whether a wife has the right to leave her husband and children – or unmentionable diseases – or local politics. I have provisionally entitled it *The Wild Duck.* It will shock some of my admirers, for it questions the preaching of ideals, which I have hitherto advocated. The Italian air and the pleasant way of life down here greatly increase my eagerness to create. We enjoyed our years in Dresden and Munich, but we are happiest in Italy.

NARRATOR: Strindberg, by contrast, had so far failed in the theatre. He had completed ten plays, but although most of them had been performed, the only good one, *Master Olof,* written when he was twenty-three, had had to wait nine years for its premiere, and his one real success had been with a pot-boiler which he rightly despised called *Lucky Peter's Journey.* He had turned his back on the theatre in disgust, as he was to do repeatedly throughout his career, and was concentrating instead on writing novels, poetry and polemical tracts. His great plays lay in the future.

IBSEN: (*Reading a letter.*) Suzannah.

SUZANNAH: (*Enters.*) Yes, Ibsen?

IBSEN: Bjoernson writes asking me to meet August Strindberg.

SUZANNAH: Is Strindberg in Rome? I'd heard he's just set up house in Switzerland.

IBSEN: Apparently he's on his way here. With his wife and children.

SUZANNAH: She's an actress, isn't she?

IBSEN: Not a good one, Bjoernson says.

SUZANNAH: What does he say about Strindberg?

IBSEN: He seems to have fallen for him. (*Laughs drily.*) Listen to this. 'Strindberg is a splendid fellow, deeply honest. Jonas Lie and I have both fallen completely in love with him. He is as noble a nature as one could wish to find'. Hm! 'His wife doesn't want to stay abroad long because she wants to go home and act in comedies. Swedes here say that she can't, that she hasn't the grace or the voice, too dry, for the stage. Strindberg thinks she

has considerable talent and is being blocked because he
has offended people in high places.'

SUZANNAH: I've heard that he's impossible.

IBSEN: They say that about me. He sounds intriguing.
I like to meet young people. One needs to know what
the next generation is thinking.

SUZANNAH: You didn't like those last two plays of his
you read. *Lucky Peter's Journey, Sir Bengt's Wife* –

IBSEN: They're rubbish, but interesting rubbish. Full of
elementary faults. He doesn't know how to construct a
play, or end it. Half his characters he doesn't bother
about. All his women are sentimentally idealised. But
he's got a mind and he knows how to write dialogue.
If only he'd stop trying to prove points.

SUZANNAH: It was the same with that novel of his.

IBSEN: *The Red Room?*

(*SUZANNAH nods.*)

Yes. All that sociological analysis. He can't analyse,
that's his weakness. He should stick to dramatising.

SUZANNAH: I thought some of the comic scenes were
very funny. That one where the young artists tear up the
floorboards of their apartment to make a fire and keep
themselves warm.

IBSEN: (*Laughs.*) And read out recipes from a cookery book
to make up for having nothing to eat. And that episode
in the brothel. Yes, he's an odd mixture of contradictions.
Let's have a look at him. If you can't stick him, you can
take his wife for a walk and leave him to me.

SUZANNAH: I wonder what he thinks of you.

STRINDBERG: (*Depressed.*) We are in Italy, but the weather
is practically Swedish. We've searched in vain for the
famous Italian blue, in both sky and water. Humbug, sir!
The olive trees are horribly grey. The landscape's not as
beautiful as you'd expect from the paintings. All these
pine trees, they're the same everywhere. And the people!
Moleskin and slouch hats! Not at all picturesque, old
chap! The houses are daubed with red, green and
yellow. The whole coast is so cluttered with wharves and

factories that one can't get to the beach. And the hills are covered with villas. Nature is dead here. No walks possible. The roads dusty. Oh, how dusty it is here! But we press on. (*Pause.*) My marriage is completely happy. Siri is as perfect a wife as one could wish for. Of course she will not be able to continue her acting career while we are abroad, but confidentially I will not be displeased at this. There are so many temptations for a working actress. You know what I mean. And being without her in the evenings when she is playing is not much fun. And she is always so tired when she gets back. We expect our third child next month. Perhaps this time it will be the son we long for.

Here we are. Via Capo le Case. Well, this is it. God, Siri, I'm scared.

SIRI: How do you think I feel?

STRINDBERG: If he doesn't like me, what shall I do?

SIRI: Don't worry, August. You'll charm him.

STRINDBERG: I doubt if he's susceptible to charm. Or his wife. She's said to be a great feminist. Of course that'll suit you. You and she will get on.

SIRI: You promised we wouldn't quarrel today.

STRINDBERG: I'm not quarrelling. I just said you and she would get on. What's wrong with that?

SIRI: Nothing. I'm sorry.

STRINDBERG: (*Morosely.*) Well.

(*Pause.*)

SIRI: Do you want me to ring the bell?

STRINDBERG: You think I'm afraid to?

SIRI: No, August.

STRINDBERG: (*Takes a deep breath.*) Here we go. (*Rings bell. Pause.*) They're not in. He's changed his mind. I knew he would. He's scared of me. Bloody old coward!

SUZANNAH: (*Formidable but courteous.*) Good morning.

STRINDBERG: (*Taken aback.*) Good morning. August Strindberg. My wife, Siri.

SUZANNAH: Fru Ibsen. You found your way?

STRINDBERG: Yes. Are we late?

SUZANNAH: (*Leads them in.*) Come this way. This is my husband.

IBSEN: (*Drily formal, looks STRINDBERG up and down before speaking.*) Ibsen.

STRINDBERG: (*Nervously formal.*) Strindberg. My wife, Siri.

SIRI: Good morning.

SUZANNAH: Please sit down.

STRINDBERG/SIRI: Thank you.

SUZANNAH: A glass of wine? Or tea?

STRINDBERG: (*Simultaneously.*) Wine, please.

SIRI: (*Simultaneously.*) Tea, please. No, wine.

SUZANNAH: (*Pours it out.*) We did not realise your condition, Fru Strindberg. These stairs must have tired you.

SIRI: A little. But I am used to stairs. August always likes to live high up.

STRINDBERG: You like to live high up.

SIRI: (*Meekly.*) Yes.

(*Awkward pause.*)

IBSEN: You are not as I had imagined you, Herr Strindberg.

STRINDBERG: (*Defensively.*) In what way?

IBSEN: So softly spoken, and so neatly dressed. From your writing I had expected someone rather fierce and Bohemian, like your young people in *The Red Room.*

STRINDBERG: Ah. Yes. Well, I can't see why having strong opinions need preclude one from dressing well.

SIRI: He spends half an hour each morning tying his cravat.

STRINDBERG: Siri –

SUZANNAH: (*Tactfully.*) Ibsen is the same. It takes him over an hour to dress each morning.

IBSEN: (*Genially.*) If one is a real revolutionary, one doesn't need to dress like one.

SUZANNAH: I always tell Ibsen he dresses like a financier.

IBSEN: People said that of Flaubert. (*Laughs.*) In the Tyrol last summer, some of the local people took me for a priest and asked for my blessing.

(*The others laugh.*)

I admired your *Red Room.*

STRINDBERG: So I have heard. I am honoured. You were my earliest inspiration. It was reading *Brand* that made me determine to become a writer.

IBSEN: *I* am honoured.

STRINDBERG: I shall never forget that evening. I was just twenty, a student at Uppsala. I felt restless, useless, crushed. And suddenly, here was someone raising his fingers at the whole Establishment and saying 'Fuck you all!'

SIRI: August!

STRINDBERG: (*Continues, regardless.*) 'You, the Government, you the Church, you our teachers, you our parents, fuck the lot of you!' Here at last was a character I could really identify with, a fanatic who dared to think that he was right and the rest of the world wrong! No half-measures, just bash on, wrench down everything that stands in your way, because you alone are right. That's what Savonarola must have sounded like when he defied the Inquisition. They burned Savonarola, but they can't burn you, not even your books.

IBSEN: I hear you don't like all my plays.

STRINDBERG: No. I didn't go for *Peer Gynt.* I just found it obscure. And *Love's Comedy* – I thought that was disgusting. Pretending that love and marriage are incompatible because love always dies, so don't marry the person you love. Love needn't die. Our love hasn't died, has it, Siri?

SIRI: No.

STRINDBERG: But *Ghosts*! My God! Having the courage to talk openly about syphilis. And say that incest need not be a sin.

IBSEN: I never actually mentioned syphilis or incest.

STRINDBERG: But everyone knew what you were talking about.

SUZANNAH: Were you ever an actor, Herr Strindberg?

STRINDBERG: It was my first ambition.

IBSEN: Indeed?

STRINDBERG: I tried. But I soon realised I had no talent. Could I have some more wine, please? And the rubbish they put on, and the way they acted! They didn't act, they declaimed. And they hardly ever looked at each other, or listened.

IBSEN: It was the same in Norway. Still is.

SIRI: Were you an actor, Herr Ibsen?

IBSEN: (*Laughs.*) Never. Not even as an amateur. No. But I was a director. How many years, Suzannah?

SUZANNAH: Twelve.

IBSEN: Twelve. First in Bergen, then in Christiania.

SIRI: So long?

IBSEN: It seemed longer.

STRINDBERG: Did you like directing?

IBSEN: (*Vehemently.*) I hated it.

SIRI: Why?

IBSEN: (*Pauses, unwilling to recall.*) Partly for the reason you mentioned. The actors didn't want to know. They didn't want to act relationships, they were only interested in themselves and their own performances. And relationships is what drama is all about.

SIRI: Couldn't you persuade them otherwise?

IBSEN: I was too timid.

STRINDBERG: Timid – you?

IBSEN: I never was a brave man face to face. And the audiences didn't want to know either. All they wanted was to be entertained.

STRINDBERG: Yes.

IBSEN: Musicals and burlesques, that kind of rubbish. Can you imagine me directing musicals and burlesques? But I had to. My biggest success was with a musical called *Fun in the Army*. Whenever I tried to give them something a little deeper, they didn't want to know. Once I tried to stage a Shakespeare play, *As You Like It*. A comedy, for heaven's sake. We had to take it off after two performances.

STRINDBERG: What about your own plays?

(*Pause.*)

SUZANNAH: They hated them most of all.

IBSEN: Well, they weren't very good, those first eight or nine I wrote. Nobody does them now, even in Norway.

I wouldn't recommend anyone to put them on. (*Laughs.*) They were hissed and booed.

SIRI: Why, Herr Ibsen?

IBSEN: Oh, because the characters weren't heroes or villains. I wanted to show that the dividing line between good and evil isn't a kind of rope with some on one side and the rest on the other. It's something that cuts through the middle of each one of us. No one is black or white, we're all differing shades of grey.

STRINDBERG: Yes.

IBSEN: Everyone accepts this in novels. But in the theatre they don't want such subtleties. Even though that's how all the great dramatists wrote. Shakespeare and the Greeks.

STRINDBERG: What about your subject matter? Did that offend them too?

IBSEN: Oh, yes. When I tried to state a few home truths about marriage – things everyone knows and that novelists have said for years – my own theatre refused to stage it.

STRINDBERG: *Love's Comedy.*

IBSEN: Yes. My wife and I were excommunicated. People avoided us in the streets. And that was in Christiania, the capital, not some little provincial town. Well, nothing could be more provincial than Christiania.

STRINDBERG: Stockholm is no better.

SIRI: Weren't you ever tempted to give up writing for the theatre?

IBSEN: Oh, I did.

STRINDBERG: I – didn't know that.

IBSEN: When I left Norway – how long ago is that, Suzannah?

SUZANNAH: Twenty years, this month.

IBSEN: I vowed I'd never write for the theatre again.
I would return to my first two loves, painting and poetry.

STRINDBERG: You paint too? I didn't know that either. So do I. Not professionally, of course. Do you paint still?

IBSEN: No.

SUZANNAH: He wasn't a very good painter.

SIRI: I'm sure that's not true.

IBSEN: No, Suzannah is right. I see that now.

STRINDBERG: You say you vowed never to write for the theatre again? But surely, you wrote *Brand* as soon as you came to Italy?

IBSEN: Not for the theatre.

STINDBERG: How do you mean?

IBSEN: I began it as a poem. (*Laughs.*) An epic poem. I completed fifty pages.

STRINDBERG: So much?

IBSEN: The best poetry I'd ever written. But that summer I came to a stop. I couldn't write another line. I'd never experienced that kind of block before. Then one day I wandered into St. Peter's, and as I was looking up at the roof of the Sistine Chapel, suddenly what I had to say and how I had to say it appeared to me with absolute clarity. I threw away the fifty pages of my poem, and started to rewrite it as a play. But as a play only to be read, not to be acted. And that meant that because I was writing for readers and not for those idiotic audiences, and idiotic actors, I could create characters, and relationships, of the same depth and complexity as though I was writing a six hundred page novel.

SIRI: Why didn't you write it as a novel?

IBSEN: I had to write it as a play. I'm not like you, Herr Strindberg. You can write novels and short stories and political tracts. I can only write plays. Poetry too once, but I gave that up. *Brand* has still never been acted. It probably never will be.

STRINDBERG: But then you went back to writing plays for the theatre.

IBSEN: Not at once.

STRINDBERG: But *Peer Gynt* –

IBSEN: I didn't write that to be performed either. Only to be read.

STRINDBERG: But it has been acted.

IBSEN: After seven years. That Swede who came to run the Christiania Theatre – Josephson –

STRINDBERG: Ludvig Josephson, yes. (*Disapprovingly.*)
The Jew. He was the one who staged my *Master Olof.*
Eventually. What sort of job did he do on *Peer Gynt?*

IBSEN: I never saw it. I was abroad. He got Grieg to write
music for it.

SIRI: What do you think of the music?

IBSEN: Grieg didn't like the play and I don't like the
music. But we're still good friends. Oh, it's fine as music,
but it turns the play into a jolly romp. It's meant to be an
uncomfortable piece. Grieg sends everyone home happy.
Well, that's the way he is.

STRINDBERG: So you had years of failure too. I didn't
realise.

IBSEN: I was a failure till I was thirty-six. You have found
success sooner than I did. Why did you give up plays to
write novels?

STRINDBERG: Because I'd failed as a playwright.

IBSEN: *Master Olof* is a fine play.

STRINDBERG: You've read it? I think so too, but it was
rejected for nine years. By the time it got put on I'd
turned to novels. Nine years! I was twenty-three when
I wrote it, thirty-two when I first saw it, a different
person. When I think of what I might have written if it
had been accepted at once! I knew it was good, I'd put
my heart and soul into that play. And I'd learned
everything from you. I modelled Olof on Brand – a
young priest who shook his fist at authority and ended
up getting beaten by the system. And you'd shown in *The
Pretenders* how to write a historical play so as to make it
relevant to modern problems. In ordinary prose, the way
they must have spoken then, the same as now.

SUZANNAH: Was that why they rejected it?

STRINDBERG: Partly. They told me tragedies had to be
written in verse.
(*IBSEN laughs.*)
They complained that I'd made giants of history talk like
people in the street. How do they suppose they talked?
Of course they didn't like the political message either.

(*Laughs.*) I rewrote it twice to try and satisfy them, I was so desperate to see it staged. Once even in verse. But they still rejected it. So then I wrote less controversial stuff which I thought they might put on, pot-boilers, and they did, and one or two had a sort of success. But if they'd staged *Master Olof* when I wrote it, my God, what plays I might have written then. I told a painter friend of mine, imagine if you'd painted what you knew was a masterpiece and you had to roll it up and stuff it in an attic for nine years. That's what happened to me.

IBSEN: But Josephson staged it two years ago and it was admired. Didn't that make you want to return to playwriting?

STRINDBERG: I have written a couple of plays since then. But they're rubbish.

IBSEN: Why?

STRINDBERG: I wrote one called *Lucky Peter's Journey* because I needed some money. The other – (*Stops.*)

IBSEN: Yes?

(*Pause.*)

STRINDBERG: I wanted to write a play in which the leading part was a woman's. For Siri. *Sir Bengt's Wife.* It's about a young woman in the sixteenth-century who – (*Is silent for a moment.*) Well, it's about marriage.

IBSEN: Always a good subject, if honestly treated.

STRINDBERG: (*Ambivalently.*) Yes.

IBSEN: So why do you call it rubbish?

STRINDBERG: It wasn't rubbish really. It just didn't work.

IBSEN: Why?

STRINDBERG: I'm not sure.

(*Pause.*)

SIRI: It was about our marriage.

IBSEN: Ah.

STRINDBERG: I wrote it as a riposte to *A Doll's House.* (*IBSEN laughs.*)

As a plea for female emancipation. I agree with you about that. I believe a woman should have the same rights as a man. That she should be allowed to keep her own name after marriage, and have her own bedroom with her own key to the door and the right to lock it. I've said all this in print. But I don't think a wife should leave her husband and children. Least of all her children.

SUZANNAH: What happens in the end of the play?

STRINDBERG: She tries to kill herself, but fails, and is – reunited with her husband. (*Pause.*) It isn't really about our marriage, we've never – of course, we've had small disagreements, as happens in every marriage – (*Laughs nervously.*) – even yours, I suppose – Nothing like what is shown in this play. I just didn't bring it off, I don't know why. The critics said it was sentimental. (*Bitterly.*) Siri had a big success. The play didn't.

SUZANNAH: But now you will write more plays?

STRINDBERG: No! I want to write about topical things – the kind of things people argue about in newspapers and debating societies and on street corners. Yes, I know you've written plays about them. But –

IBSEN: Yes?

STRINDBERG: Oh, you can be so damned objective about it all? You can see both sides. I don't, I can't pretend to, I get angry and then I get sentimental. Anger's all right in books, it doesn't seem to work in the theatre.

IBSEN: I was angry when I wrote *A Doll's House* and *Ghosts.* And *An Enemy of the People.*

STRINDBERG: Yes, but you can control your anger and channel it. I can't. No, I know I can't, and it's no use trying. And – oh, I know you'll think this stupid, but I can't portray a woman unsympathetically. Minor characters, yes, the main one, no.

SUZANNAH: Why is that?

STRINDBERG: (*Simply.*) I idealise women. (*Pause.*) My mother died when I was thirteen. Ever since then I've always put women on a pedestal. I want a woman I can worship. But then – well, naturally, I desire her, and then I despise her for letting me…and myself for…violating my image of her. Does this shock you?

SUZANNAH: No.

STRINDBERG: Well, one can't put that kind of thing on the stage.

IBSEN: Why not?

STRINDBERG: No manager would touch it. (*Laughs.*) One would have to start one's own theatre. And you need a lot of money to do that. No, to get plays put on you've got to compromise. I'm sorry, I don't mean that personally. What you did in *Ghosts* was brave and splendid. But I can't channel my emotions. I have to say things straight. That's difficult enough with a book, I keep having to change publishers. But to say it in a play – I'd be wasting my time, and I can't afford that, we've two children and a third on the way, I'm always in debt as it is. I have to write things that will pay bills. Tell me, what made you give up writing big plays in verse, like *Brand* and *Peer Gynt*, for plays with five or six people in a single room, like *A Doll's House* and *Ghosts*?

IBSEN: You know how it is. Hitherto, tragedy has always been written on an epic scale – the way I wrote *The Pretenders* and you *Master Olof.* Lots of characters and lots of different scenes. And always kings and queens, or princes and princesses, or at the lowest Montagues and Capulets. I wanted to show – what everyone knows – that most tragedies occur in small rooms, among people called Mr and Mrs, talking ordinary simple prose.

STRINDBERG: Tragedy in a small room. Yes, that might be something for me.

SIRI: (*Not meaning anything.*) It would suit you.

STRINDBERG: What do you mean by that?

SIRI: I didn't mean anything, August.

IBSEN: (*Quickly.*) There was something else I wanted to change. You will have noticed it, though most people still haven't. That boring old convention by which every plot has to be shunted along by means of overheard conversations and intercepted letters and mistaken identities. When I began to write I used these because every dramatist before me had done so. Critics said I had borrowed this from that French writer Scribe.

75

Haven't they read Shakespeare or the Greeks? I can't
think of a play by them which doesn't depend on such
things.

STRINDBERG: That's true. I hadn't thought of that.
Overheard conversations, intercepted letters, mistaken
identities. Yes, it can't be easy to make a play go forward
without those.

IBSEN: It's not so hard once you stop depending on them.

SUZANNAH: I must prepare lunch.

SIRI: May I help you?

SUZANNAH: There's no need, I can easily manage.

SIRI: I'd like to.

SUZANNAH: You're very kind. Thank you. You men go
for a walk. Show Herr Strindberg the gardens.
(*The men go.*)

SIRI: Herr Ibsen is so unlike what I had imagined.

SUZANNAH: In what way?

SIRI: I'd heard he was very silent and difficult to bring out.

SUZANNAH: He's like that in large gatherings. He hates
big parties. Or if he doesn't like someone, then he says
nothing. He likes you and your husband. He expected to.

SIRI: We were afraid he wouldn't. August is so fierce, he
wants to pull everything down.

SUZANNAH: So did Ibsen when he was your husband's age.

SIRI: Why do you always call him by his surname?

SUZANNAH: Most women of my generation address their
husbands like that. Didn't your mother?

SIRI: No. But she was very unconventional. She wrote
poetry. She'd have liked to have had a career. She envied
me mine. Not that I have a career just now.

SUZANNAH: That is only while you are abroad.

SIRI: But how long shall we stay abroad? August says he
writes better away from Sweden because the pressure is
less. They hate him so much in Sweden.

SUZANNAH: It was the same with us in Norway. Ibsen
doesn't want to go back and live there. He's hated it
every time we've returned. We may have to, though.

SIRI: Why?

SUZANNAH: Our son is twenty-four. He wants to go into
politics. That would have to be in Norway, of course.
And Ibsen wouldn't want to live far from him. They're
very close. So I suppose we shall end our days there.

SIRI: Didn't you ever want a career of your own, Fru Ibsen?

SUZANNAH: Oh, yes.

SIRI: What?

SUZANNAH: I wanted to write.

SIRI: What kind of things?

SUZANNAH: Novels. And plays. I was regarded as very
advanced in my views. Especially on female emancipation.

SIRI: Why didn't you?

SUZANNAH: (*Laughs.*) If you're married to a great writer,
it's difficult to write yourself.

SIRI: But he wasn't a great writer yet. Not till long after
you'd married, surely?

SUZANNAH: Oh, he was great all right, even then. He
hadn't found himself yet, that was all.

SIRI: But –

SUZANNAH: No, being a wife to Ibsen was a full-time job.
He had no real belief in himself. You look surprised.
He'd had failure after failure, and they continued. And
he was a failure as a director too, as he told you. It was
bad enough in Bergen, but worse when we moved to
Christiania. If I hadn't forced him to write, he'd have
given it up. Yes, I promise you. And by the time he'd
succeeded – How could I write my little books in one
room while Ibsen was writing *Brand* and *Peer Gynt* in the
other?

SIRI: Don't you regret it? The children you might have
had? August always thinks of books as children.

SUZANNAH: Ibsen's plays are my children, as much as
our son is.

SIRI: I see.

SUZANNAH: You couldn't do the same?

SIRI: For August? No, it isn't enough for me. If I'd wanted
to be a writer, perhaps. I might feel I was fulfilling
myself as a part-author of his plays and novels, the way

you do. But I'm an actress. It's the only thing I can do.
And my career has been killed. I can't act in French and
German. I'm nearly thirty-four. When he wooed me, he
wrote such marvellous letters, he said he would write
plays for me that would make me the greatest actress in
the land. But when I had a success, in *Sir Bengt's Wife*, it
made him jealous. I got good reviews, and he bad ones.
And he's so – so insanely suspicious, he thought I was
having an affair with every actor I worked with.

SUZANNAH: Some men are like that.

SIRI: And I was earning more than he was, and that hurt his
pride. He wants to be the breadwinner. That was one
reason why he wanted to go abroad. I sometimes think it
was the main reason. He didn't want to become known as
the husband of the actress.

SUZANNAH: You have a hard cross to bear.

SIRI: I don't know how much longer I can bear it.

(*The men are heard coming.*)

SUZANNAH: We must get on.

(*They go. The men enter.*)

IBSEN: What else have you seen in Rome, Herr
Strindberg?

STRINDBERG: Not much yet. We only got in last night.
We've just had time to visit the Sistine Chapel.

IBSEN: Ah!

STRINDBERG: That Last Judgement of Michelangelo.
It's sublime. I'd only seen engravings of it. My God,
fancy being able to see God like that!

IBSEN: I owe more to him than anyone.

STRINDBERG: God, or Michelangelo?

IBSEN: (*Laughs.*) Michelangelo. The smart critics disparage
him. They call him extravagant and barbaric. They say
the same about Shakespeare, of course.

STRINDBERG: Bloody idiots.

IBSEN: The painter they want us to admire is Raphael.
(*Contemptuously.*) Harmony and reconciliation. Well, it
ties up with conventional religious thinking, If you think
all's well with the world, that God marks the fall of a
sparrow, Raphael's your man.

STRINDBERG: Yet there's a kind of calm in
Michelangelo's figures.

IBSEN: But it's the calm of someone who has fought with
chaos and despair. Have you been to Florence?

STRINDBERG: Not yet.

IBSEN: In the Boboli Gardens there, stand Michelangelo's
unfinished statues. I find them even more powerful than
his completed masterpieces. Men and women straining to
free themselves from the marble that imprisons them. He
created in stone what I wanted to create in words. Men
and women seeking to liberate themselves from the trolls
that bind them. The trolls within, as well as the trolls
without.

STRINDBERG: Ghosts.

IBSEN: Yes. And when I was stuck with *Brand*, it was his
Last Judgement that showed me the way I had to go.

STRINDBERG: Surely you aren't religious?

IBSEN: I try not to be.

STRINDBERG: (*Incredulous.*) You have doubts? You, of all
men?

IBSEN: You have none?

STRINDBERG: Surely one must fight such doubts! Religion
is a deception, a fraud. It teaches men to be passive, to
unload responsibility on to Christ and the Church. Opium
for the masses, Karl Marx called it. Have you read *Das
Kapital* ?

IBSEN: My wife has read it and told me what it contains.
She understands that kind of abstract writing better than
I do.

STRINDBERG: Of course I was brought up religious. My
parents were Pietists. Very strict. It took me years to free
myself. How can people read Charles Darwin and still
believe that the Bible is the Word of God? Genesis has
been proved a lie and that's only Chapter One. And now
some Frenchman has written a historical life of Christ
proving that the New Testament isn't all true either.

IBSEN: I felt as you do. My mother was deeply religious.
But I determined to be a freethinker, like you. The

church's teaching seemed to me humbug. I still think so.
But that does not mean that religion is humbug.

STRINDBERG: (*Sceptically.*) Belief in a God? All that
rubbish with wafers and wine?

IBSEN: Belief in something. I'm beginning to find that one
can't just give up religion. It leaves a gap which needs to
be filled.

STRINDBERG: With what?

IBSEN: I'm not sure.

SUZANNAH: (*Enters with SIRI.*) Gentlemen – the food is
ready, if you would like to come through.
(*They all go. Fade lights. Music. Lights up. They all enter.*)

STRINDBERG: My word, that was good. God, how I've
missed Scandinavian food. This was the first I've eaten in
six months.

SUZANNAH: Do you not cook Scandinavian food, Fru
Strindberg?

SIRI: August likes to eat *en pension.*

STRINDBERG: Siri wasn't brought up to cook. These
aristocrats, you know. We've suffered a good deal in
France and Switzerland. Filthy muck they serve there.

IBSEN: (*Drily.*) Really?

STRINDBERG: All that garlic they put in everything.
Even the bread. Have you been to France?

IBSEN: Just for a couple of weeks. Fifteen years ago, on my
way to Egypt and back.

STRINDBERG: What were you doing in Egypt?

IBSEN: Your king sent me to represent Norway at the
opening of the Suez Canal.

STRINDBERG: Good heavens.

IBSEN: Well, he's our king too. It ruffled a few feathers in
Norway. He didn't know how much they hate me there.

STRINDBERG: Where were you, Paris?

IBSEN: Mostly.

STRINDBERG: What did you think of it?

IBSEN: Beautiful. I spent most of my time visiting art
galleries and museums. They have some curious new
painters there.

STRINDBERG: I should say so. We went to an exhibition by someone called Manet. I think he must have something wrong with his eyes or be touched in the head. He uses colours which don't exist in nature.

IBSEN: Yes, he didn't appeal to me.

SIRI: Did you go to the theatres at all?

IBSEN: No. I seldom visit the theatre.

STRINDBERG: We were taken to see Sarah Bernhardt in a play called *Frou-Frou*.

SUZANNAH: What was she like?

STRINDBERG: Horrible! Just tricks and mannerisms. Shit.

SIRI: August!

STRINDBERG: (*To IBSEN.*) I beg your pardon. No, she's the kind of actress we don't want. Grand opera without the music. All right for the kind of rubbish she appears in. We can do without her kind. How long do you take to write a play?

IBSEN: Three or four months. How about you?

STRINDBERG: Three or four weeks.

IBSEN: So little? How many drafts do you make?

STRINDBERG: None. I don't even read through what I've written. I just send it off to the publisher.

IBSEN: Don't read it through? Why on earth not?

STRINDBERG: One's mind is divided into two, isn't it? The creative and the critical. With me, the critical side tends to dominate. It keeps telling me: 'That won't do.' I found it got in the way, so now I write as fast as I can and throw each page on the floor as I finish it. When it's done Siri gathers it up and posts it off.

IBSEN: Amazing.

STRINDBERG: I write like a sleepwalker. My brain works ceaselessly, it grinds and grinds like a mill and I can't stop. I find no rest till I've got it down on paper. But then something new starts at once and the misery begins again.

IBSEN: What about inconsistencies?

STRINDBERG: I rely on the publisher to iron them out. I reckon I gain in spontaneity what I lose in tidying up details. And I trust the impulsive side of my nature more than I do the critical side. Things stay in which I'd be scared of leaving if I read it through. How many drafts do you write?

IBSEN: Three, as a rule.

STRINDBERG: So many?

IBSEN: Yes. I brood on the characters for weeks before I start. I have to get them fixed in my mind, to penetrate to the last wrinkle of their souls. How they stand and walk, what their voices sound like, what they wear, to the last button.

STRINDBERG: Then you know all about them before you even start to write?

IBSEN: Oh, no. When I begin my first draft, I know them as one knows people with whom one has shared a railway carriage on a longish journey. One has made a preliminary acquaintance, chatted about this and that. By the time I have written the second draft I know them as one would know fellow-guests after a month in a spa at the same hotel. And after my final draft, I really know them, they have no secrets from me.

STRINDBERG: I wonder if I shall ever work like that. I'm so dead scared of the critic in me, I don't think I shall ever dare to write except the way I do now. It means I turn out a lot of rubbish, of course. But if I tried to write the way you do, I don't think I'd ever finish anything.

IBSEN: You must do what is best for you. It means you will be able to write things that I couldn't.

STRINDBERG: Perhaps.

IBSEN: Tell me, how many of the plays you've written have been historical?

STRINDBERG: Let me think. (*Pause.*) Seven. Out of ten.

IBSEN: So many? Why is that, I wonder?

STRINDBERG: I don't know really.

IBSEN: I ask because you are so actively interested in the present. Your other writings show that. Politics, and social problems, and the relationship between the sexes.

I followed the same pattern when I was young, most of my early plays were historical. Well, audiences expected that. They didn't want to see their own problems presented on the stage except behind a gauze of history so that they could pretend it didn't really concern them.

STRINDBERG: What about *Love's Comedy?*

IBSEN: Look what happened to that.

STRINDBERG: *Brand*?

IBSEN: That was only for reading.

STRINDBERG: *The League of Youth?*

IBSEN: They accepted that because I wrote it as a kind of farce. And then the fact that it exposed a certain kind of left-winger whom I despise, the kind that gives his party – our party – a bad name, that made people accept it for the wrong reason. The first serious modern play I tried to write, *The Pillars of Society*, gave me endless trouble. I made notes for it, dropped it for three or four years, went back to it, dropped it again for two years – it took me over seven years to write, from start to finish. There was some kind of block I had to overcome before writing a serious play with a modern setting. You may find the same.

STRINDBERG: Perhaps. But that *League of Youth*. How could you hold up your own party to ridicule like that? You've always been on the left, like me. You must have known the ammunition it would give those bloody Tories.

IBSEN: A writer must be the conscience of the party he supports. He must condemn it, publicly, every time it betrays its principles. A practising politician can't do that to the same extent.

STRINDBERG: Why not?

IBSEN: Because no politician can achieve anything on his own. Only as a member of the party. If he protests against party policy more than occasionally, he becomes a figure crying in the wilderness, brave but ineffective. So if a writer is not the conscience of his party, who will be? He must criticise it more severely than he criticises the other side, because there are others who will do that.

STRINDBERG: But then one gets damned by both sides.

IBSEN: Yes. Being a writer is a lonely business. Well, you know that. One must expect to be abused. The worst thing is being abused by one's friends.

STRINDBERG: Yes, I've found that. Can you manage without friends? I can't.

IBSEN: I have learned to.

STRINDBERG: But you're self-sufficient. I'm not. I'm gregarious, I need to meet people. But I make enemies so easily. I can't keep my mouth shut, I have to point out their faults, and then of course they hate me.

IBSEN: You'll have to learn to accept that. Friends are an expensive luxury. Or avoid controversy. But you won't want to do that. Controversy is your strength. Don't be over-sensitive to criticism.

STRINDBERG: I can't not be. I can't make myself thick-skinned. Does that mean that I shall never find peace?

IBSEN: Not necessarily.

STRINDBERG: How, then?

IBSEN: You only need one person to find peace.

STRINDBERG: The right person, yes. (*Pause.*) I have found that person. But not peace. There are certain demands – one might call them the demands of the ideal –
(*IBSEN laughs tersely.*)
Why do you laugh?

IBSEN: That's exactly the line I'm putting into the mouth of one of the characters in my new play.

STRINDBERG: Does he find the answer?

IBSEN: No.

STRINDBERG: But you have always preached the importance of ideals.

IBSEN: Yes. But ideals are not for everyone. They are for the few.

STRINDBERG: What about the others?

IBSEN: They have to live on illusions. They have to find a life-lie, and believe that.

SIRI: A life-lie?

STRINDBERG: That would never be enough for me.
I must hunt the truth, even if it destroys me.

SUZANNAH: Then you are destined to more than the
usual measure of human suffering.

STRINDBERG: I have begun to feel that. Sometimes
I think that I will only find happiness – what am I saying?
fulfilment – in taking an active part in revolution.

IBSEN: Manning the barricades? Have you the courage?

STRINDBERG: I shall have to find out. Have you?

IBSEN: No. I never had physical courage. I envy those who
have. But I don't believe in revolutions.

STRINDBERG: But everything I have ever read by you
demands revolution.

IBSEN: Revolution, yes. Revolutions, no. There is a big
difference. Revolutions always fail, political revolutions
I mean. They always throw up a new tyrant as bad as or
worse than the tyrant who caused the revolution. Name
me one exception.
(*STRINDBERG is silent.*)
The only revolution that matters is the revolution of the
spirit of man. When a man says: 'I will not obey the
Church', like Luther or Savonarola, or: 'I will not obey
this unjust law' and goes to the gallows for it, or when a
woman has the courage to leave her husband – (*Stops.*)

SUZANNAH: Another cup of coffee, Fru Strindberg?

SIRI: Thank you. Yes, I would like one.

STRINDBERG: Siri would never wish to leave me. Or our
children. God forbid.

IBSEN: I am sure. But sometimes –

STRINDBERG: Let us leave this subject, please. I find it
distasteful. I am bothered at what you said just now, that
political revolutions must fail. I have met Russian
nihilists in Switzerland. They are brave and splendid
men, who seek to overthrow a tyranny, that is all they
live for and they are ready to die for it. Is that not
worthwhile?

IBSEN: It is a brave aim. But if they succeed, that will only
lead to another tyranny in their country, perhaps worse.

STRINDBERG: And yet one must strive for something.

IBSEN: Yes! For self-liberation. Man cannot be liberated from without, only from within.

STRINDBERG: Kierkegaard.

IBSEN: (*Smiles.*) So I am told. That was what I was trying to say in *A Doll's House*, though few people perceived it. They think it's a play about female emancipation.

SIRI: (*Indignant.*) What is it about, if not that?

IBSEN: Something much bigger. Human emancipation. The need for every individual, be he man or be she woman, to find out who he or she really is and to become that person. Hardly anyone does. The Church is largely to blame. Luther was right when he said that every man must face God alone. But the Protestant Church has long since abandoned that ideal.

STRINDBERG: But must I always be persecuted? People say I have an obsession about this. It isn't an obsession. I am persecuted.

IBSEN: You will always be persecuted, as I have been. We belong to those who have troubled the sleep of the world, and so cannot expect objectivity or tolerance.

SIRI: August, we must go. The children will be missing us.

STRINDBERG: (*Gently.*) Yes, you are right. The children. What would one do without them? They are the best that life has to offer.

IBSEN: I agree.

STRINDBERG: It has been most kind of you to receive us. You have confused me. Very much. But I am grateful for it. And for the lunch.

SIRI: Goodbye. Thank you – both.

(*They remain seated.*)

NARRATOR: No such conversation as this ever took place. Strindberg did indeed set out to meet Ibsen in Rome that spring of 1884, but the weather in North Italy was so bad that he lost heart at Genoa and returned home to Switzerland. He and Ibsen were destined never to meet. By the end of the year, Strindberg's relations with Siri reached breaking-point. He accused her, among other things, of being a Lesbian, and she, being devout, found his increasingly obsessive atheism impossible to bear. For the children's sake she stayed with him for another eight years. Their fraught marriage caused him to abandon politics and sociology and concentrate on writing about the sex war, which resulted in his greatest plays, such as *The Father, Miss Julie, Creditors* and *The Dance of Death*. He remarried twice, with much younger women, but these marriages likewise ended in disaster. Siri never remarried, and died in poverty. (*Pause. SIRI goes.*) Nor did Ibsen's peace of mind last much longer. Five years later, when he was sixty-one, an eighteen year old Viennese girl named Emilie Bardach fell passionately in love with him, and he with her. They agreed to go away together, but for reasons which we can only guess at – an old man's fear of not being able to satisfy, or keep satisfied, a young girl; fear of scandal; unwillingness to leave Suzannah, on whom he was so dependent – he reneged on the agreement and never saw Emilie again.

(*SUZANNAH goes.*)

The five final plays which he wrote after this encounter – *Hedda Gabler, The Master Builder, Little Eyolf, John Gabriel Borkman* and *When We Dead Awaken* – are his blackest and, in many people's view, his greatest. (*Pause.*) As Strindberg's marriage began to crumble, Women, with a capital W, became The Great Enemy, on whom he blamed everything; and Ibsen, for having encouraged them with *A Doll's House*, the worst enemy of all. Within four months of setting out to meet him in Rome, Strindberg was describing Ibsen as 'swinish'.

STRINDBERG: (*Hysterical, but quietly rational.*) Ibsen's spirit is sick and aging. He has nothing to teach me. He is an ignorant women's writer. He speaks only for women and the young, and is consequently hated by grown men. That is why I hate him, the more so since he caused the Young to rebel, together with Married Women, against Men who are the Lords of Creation. (*Pause.*) This new play of Ibsen's, *Hedda Gabler*, is a

blatant crib of my *Miss Julie*. (*Laughs.*) My seed has fallen
into Ibsen's brainpan and fertilised. Now he carries my
seed and is my uterus. He has based his character of
Eilert Löevborg, the drunken genius, on me, personally.
But his shit will rebound on him! For I shall survive
him... The war I have waged against Ibsen for five years
has cost me my wife, children, fortune and career. He is
one of the three worst humbugs of the age, with Wagner
and Pasteur.

NARRATOR: Ibsen's admiration of Strindberg never
waned. He praised him publicly as 'a very great talent',
and after his return to Norway he bought a full-length
portrait of Strindberg which he hung on his study wall.
When a visitor expressed surprise on seeing this, Ibsen
muttered:

IBSEN: A remarkable man.

The End.

THE SUMMER IN GOSSENSASS

Characters

HENRIK IBSEN

SUZANNAH IBSEN
his wife

EMILIE BARDACH

FRAU BARDACH
her mother

LINA
the Ibsen's maid

HELENE RAFF

HEDDA GABLER

EJLERT LÖVBORG

A GENTLEMAN FRIEND

The Summer in Gossensass was commissioned by the British Broadcasting Corporation as a fictionalised documentary, and was shown on BBC 1 on 15 September 1964, with the following cast:

HENRIK IBSEN/HAKVARD SOLNESS, Claes Gill

SUZANNAH IBSEN, Molly Urquhart

EMILIE BARDACH/HILDE WANGEL, Camilla Hasse

FRAU BARDACH, Ingeborg Wells

HELENE RAFF, Anna Polk

HEDDA GABLER, Vivien Merchant

EJLERT LÖVBORG, John Wood

GEORGE TESSMAN, Jeffry Wickham

Directed by Casper Wrede

This stage adaptation was first performed (in Norwegian) at the Ibsen Teater, Skien, on 29 August 1998, with the following cast:

HENRIK IBSEN, Morten Borgersen

SUZANNAH IBSEN, Sylvia Salvesen

EMILIE BARDACH, Kristin Skogheim

FRAU BARDACH/LINA, Veslemoy Haslund

HELENE RAFF, Iris Johansen

NARRATOR, Mads Jorgensen

Translator/director, Terje Linberg

The action takes place in Gossensass in the Tyrol, Munich, Vienna and Christiania between 1889 and 1898

Two hotel rooms, one on either side of the stage. In one of them, a man of 61 in shirtsleeves with a cravat is writing a letter. In the other, a girl of 18 is reading a book in a dressing gown, with a towel round her head. In the distance, a brass band is playing.

IBSEN: (*Reads through his letter, softly.*) 21st July 1889, my dear Lund. Since the beginning of this month Suzannah and I have been in the Tyrol. We shall be spending the rest of the summer here. We have chosen Gossensass, where we have so often stayed before. The scenery here is magnificent and the air excellent. Gossensass stands 3,300 feet above sea level, just below the Brenner Pass and three hours rail journey from Innsbruck. This afternoon I have to attend a tedious ceremony. The town had decided to honour me by naming a little plateau on the hill above it the Ibsenplatz, because I like to sit here and look out across the valley. I dread these occasions; but I must attend. Afterwards there is to be a fête of some kind. The whole thing will be a torture for me.
(*SUZANNAH IBSEN, the same age as him, heavy and leaning on a stick, limps in carrying his dress coat. He rises silently; she holds it for him as he puts it on. She is the servant, he the master. He turns; she looks him up and down, adjusts his cravat. He inclines his head formally.*
On the other side of the stage, there is an urgent knocking on the door.)

FRAU BARDACH: (*Off.*) Emilie, Emilie!

EMILIE: What is it?

FRAU BARDACH: (*Aged 50, enters, formally dressed with a hat.*) Emilie – ! Good heavens, aren't you ready?

EMILIE. What for?

FRAU BARDACH: What for? Why, the fête.

EMILIE: What fête? (*Remembers.*) Oh, my God!

FRAU BARDACH: Emilie!

EMILIE: Oh, mother, why didn't you remind me?

FRAU BARDACH: Remind you! Why, the whole town has been thinking of nothing else for days.

EMILIE: Oh, damn, damn!

FRAU BARDACH: (*Shocked.*) Emilie!

EMILIE: Get my dress, quick.

FRAU BARDACH: You can't possibly be ready in time.
They'll be starting any minute now. They're only waiting
for him. (*Points to the window.*) Look!
(*EMILIE looks out of the window. The brass band music
grows louder.*)
I can't wait or I'll miss it.

EMILIE: No, go, go.

FRAU BARDACH: (*Consolingly.*) I'll tell you all about it.
(*EMILIE does not reply. FRAU BARDACH goes. IBSEN,
in the other room, takes up his gloves, top hat and cane, and
walks alone down the corridor past EMILIE's door.
SUZANNAH, leaning heavily on her stick, watches him; she
is too lame to take part in the procession. EMILIE in her
room hears the measured footsteps outside. She goes to the
door, waits till they have passed, then opens the door gently
and peers out. She sees his back. As though sensing that someone
is looking at him, he stops, then slowly turns his head. He sees
her in the doorway, a towel round her head, a schoolgirl
frightened at being caught in some misdemeanour. After a
moment, she quickly closes the door. He looks at it, slightly
troubled, he does not know why. The band strikes up again
outside. He turns and goes out.*)

EMILIE: The weather has been very bad, and we cannot
make any excursions. The day of the Ibsen fête has been
the only fine one. But I washed my hair and could not go
out. After the concert, however, I made his acquaintance
in a way quite delightful. I was seated alone on a bench,
reading a book, in a valley named the Pflerschtal on the
outskirts of the town.
(*She takes the towel from her head and removes her dressing-
gown, revealing ordinary clothes beneath. She walks upstage
and sits on a bench, reading her book. Back projections of
mountains. IBSEN enters; stands for a moment looking out
over the landscape; sees her and approaches. His shadow falls
over her. She looks up. He bows stiffly. She rises and drops
him a scared curtsey.*)

I'd washed my hair. (*He does not speak.*) I'd been
meaning to come. But I forgot and – washed my hair –
so I couldn't.
(*He formally inclines his head.*)
Won't you sit down?

IBSEN: Thank you, no.
(*She looks at him doubtfully for a moment, then decides on
her approach. He holds out her book to him.*)

EMILIE: Have you read this? Beaconsfield's *Endymion*.
(*No response.*)
Mama said I should. She said it was edifying.

IBSEN: I seldom read books.

EMILIE: Oh?

IBSEN: I leave them to my wife.

EMILIE: I should have thought you'd read heaps of books.
(*No response.*)
You must read something.

IBSEN: I read the newspapers.

EMILIE: Is that all?

IBSEN: It's enough. If you read every word.

EMILIE: (*Pertly.*) Including the advertisements?

IBSEN: Especially the advertisements.
(*He looks at her and his expression relaxes a little.*)
Do you often sit here?

EMILIE: Oh, yes. I like it here.

IBSEN: It's certainly a magnificent view.

EMILIE: It isn't that. I can be alone here. High up – and
alone.
(*He looks at her.*)
What's so strange about that?

IBSEN: I should have thought you'd like to be with people.
At your age. How old are you?

EMILIE: Eighteen.
(*Pause. She makes a place next to her. He sits.*)

IBSEN: What is your name?

EMILIE: Emilie.

IBSEN: Emilie what?

EMILIE: Emilie Bardach.

IBSEN: Do you live here, Fraulein Bardach?

EMILIE: Good heavens, no. (*Proudly.*) I'm from Vienna.

IBSEN: (*Indifferently.*) Ah, Vienna.

EMILIE: (*Disappointed.*) Don't you like it?

IBSEN: (*As before.*) It is a beautiful city.

EMILIE: My father says it's more beautiful even than London or St Petersburg.

IBSEN: I haven't been to London or St Petersburg.

EMILIE: Gosh! I should have imagined you'd been everywhere. You can't spend all your time up there in Sweden.

IBSEN: Norway.

EMILIE: Of course, I mean Norway.

IBSEN: No, I haven't lived there for a long time. Twenty-five years.

EMILIE: Didn't you like it there?

IBSEN: (*Smiles sternly.*) They didn't like me. So I came abroad. Then I – found it suited me to be a foreigner.

EMILIE: How?

IBSEN: I felt freer. I could think more clearly.

EMILIE: Where have you been living all these years, then?

IBSEN: Italy and Germany. Rome – Dresden – Munich. Then Rome again – and now Munich again.

EMILIE: It must have been a lot of trouble, moving your furniture and everything.

IBSEN: We have very little furniture.

EMILIE: Oh?

IBSEN: We live in rooms.

EMILIE: (*Surprised.*) Furnished rooms?

IBSEN: Yes.

EMILIE: Do you like that?

IBSEN: Yes.

EMILIE: Does you wife?

IBSEN: (*Looks at her.*) She likes what I like.

EMILIE: Is she here with you?

IBSEN: Of course.

EMILIE: What's she like?

IBSEN: (*Looks at her again, sternly.*) You ask a great many questions, young lady.

EMILIE: Well, you started asking me questions.

IBSEN: That is the privilege of age.

EMILIE: Oh, come on! Tell me!

IBSEN: (*After a pause.*) Suzannah is a remarkable woman. She is the eagle that showed me the way to the summit. (*EMILIE, awed, waits for him to continue.*) She believed in me when no one else did. When I didn't believe in myself. I was a failure till I was nearly forty, you know. A dreadful failure. Without her, I couldn't have gone on –

EMILIE: Couldn't have gone on writing?

IBSEN: Living.

(*Pause.*)

EMILIE: Why didn't she come up here with you? Oh, I suppose she's listening to the concert.

IBSEN: No, she is at the hotel. (*EMILIE looks questioningly at him.*) She can't walk very far, you see. Suzannah is lame.

EMILIE: Oh – I'm sorry. Please forgive me.

IBSEN: (*Inclines his head silently.*) Well, she is becoming old now. We are both old.

EMILIE: You're not old.

IBSEN: I'm sixty-one.

EMILIE: Perhaps. But you're not old.

IBSEN: (*Gently.*) Yes. I am.

EMILIE: No! If you'd been old, I couldn't have sat here talking to you like this. I can't stand old people. (*With sudden vehemence.*) You're young! You'll always be young! (*She puts her hand instinctively on his knee. He turns his eyes on her. She is frightened at what she sees in them and takes her hand away. Her eyes remain fixed, scared yet excited, on his, which are blazing and formidable. Suddenly they dull.*)

IBSEN: (*Very quietly.*) No. I am old. (*Takes out his watch, looks at it and puts its back.*) And now I must be going. I must be back before the concert finishes. (*Gets up and raises his hat.*) Good evening, Fraulein – er –

(*He turns and walks away.*)

EMILIE: (*Her fingers between her teeth, still held by the violence of his eyes, says half to herself.*) Frightfully exciting – !

(He hears the words and stops; seems about to turn, but does not. He goes.
The lights dim; it is evening. Back in the hotel. Waltz music. EMILIE and FRAU BARDACH seated at one side of the stage, IBSEN and SUZANNAH at the other, silent.)

FRAU BARDACH: Aren't you going to dance at all tonight, Emilie?

EMILIE: No, mother.

FRAU BARDACH: That's six times you've been asked.

EMILIE: I don't want to dance. I think I'll take a walk.

FRAU BARDACH: I really don't understand you.

EMILIE: *(Under her breath.)* No.

(A rose garden is projected. Masses of roses, everywhere. EMILIE leaves her mother and walks among the roses. She paces to and fro restlessly. Plucks a flower absently, and smells it. Then she inhales it deeply several times, closing her eyes. IBSEN leaves SUZANNAH and comes behind her as in the previous scene.)

(Aware of him, but not turning her head.) Is it you?

IBSEN: Good evening, young lady.

EMILIE: I was beginning to think you weren't coming.

IBSEN: *(A little severely.)* Was there something you wanted to say to me?

EMILIE: Nothing particular.

IBSEN: Then why did you – ?

EMILIE: You looked so bored. Among all those old people. *(Suddenly mischievous.)* Come on! Admit you were bored!

IBSEN: *(Severely again.)* I don't know why you should assume that.
(She does not speak.)
Well, yes, perhaps I was a little bored.

EMILIE: You see! I wormed it out of you in the end!

IBSEN: All the same, you shouldn't have beckoned me out like that.

EMILIE: Why not?

IBSEN: Well, people don't... *(Hesitates.)*

EMILIE: People don't do such things?

IBSEN: Exactly.

EMILIE: Oh, now you're talking exactly like one of *them*.

IBSEN: Well, I am one of them.

EMILIE: Oh, don't be so silly.

(*Pause.*)

IBSEN: It's a long time since anyone called me that.

EMILIE: Then it's time someone did. You're not one of them, any more than I am. You're the same age as me.

IBSEN: The same age – ! You are eighteen. And I am sixty-one.

EMILIE: What's that got to do with it?

(*They begin to walk among the roses.*)

IBSEN: You ought to be dancing in there. With all those handsome young men.

EMILIE: They bore me.

IBSEN: I thought one or two of them looked quite lively and intelligent.

EMILIE: (*Does not answer; then.*) You must have had heaps of mistresses.

IBSEN: I beg your pardon?

EMILIE: Well, haven't you?

IBSEN: What makes you think that?

EMILIE: You're frightfully famous. And girls fall for famous men.

IBSEN: I became famous rather late in life.

EMILIE: What's that got to do with it?

(*Pause.*)

IBSEN: You know, you're a very strange young lady, Fraulein Bardach.

EMILIE: How?

IBSEN: I can't quite make out whether you're having me on.

EMILIE: Making fun of you?

IBSEN: Yes. Making fun of me.

EMILIE: Why should I do that?

IBSEN: It's a thing some people like doing.

EMILIE: Tell me about them.

IBSEN: About whom?

EMILIE: Your mistresses.

IBSEN: That's really a rather impertinent question, you know, Fraulein Bardach.

EMILIE: I don't see why.

IBSEN: What would you think of me if I were to ask you to tell me about your lovers.

EMILIE: I haven't had any lovers. But if I had, I'd tell you about them.

IBSEN: Well, I haven't had any mistresses. Not since I married, anyway. And that was over thirty years ago. So there's nothing to tell you. And now I think we should go back to the others.

EMILIE: I don't want to go back to them.

IBSEN: But they'll be wondering where you are.

EMILIE: Let them.

IBSEN: And where I am.

EMILIE: Do you mind what other people think about you?

IBSEN: Yes.

EMILIE: Why?

IBSEN: Well, I have a kind of – position after all.

EMILIE: I wouldn't have thought you'd have cared a bit. You've never been afraid of shocking people in print. You said I was strange just now. I think you're much stranger. All your life you've been a rebel, haven't you? But you don't dress like a rebel – you dress like a banker – like Pappa. And just now you even began to talk like him.

IBSEN: Oh? What did I say that he says?

EMILIE: (*Imitates him.*) 'I have a kind of – position, after all.' Pappa says that at least twice a week.
(*Pause.*)

IBSEN: I'm beginning to get a little frightened of you, Fraulein Bardach.

EMILIE: Frightened of *me*? Why?

IBSEN: You pry into my secrets. People don't usually question me like this. I'm not sure that I like it.

EMILIE: I thought you were so keen on everyone knowing the truth about themselves. Didn't one of your characters say that nobody had the right to an illusion?

IBSEN: Oh, you've read that play, have you? But he destroyed everyone around him.

EMILIE: But it's what you believe.

IBSEN: No. (*Pause.*) I believe that certain people can't live without illusions.

EMILIE: But you're not one of them, are you?

IBSEN: And suppose I am not?

EMILIE: Didn't you once also say that whatever people turn their backs on gets them in the end?

IBSEN: I don't remember ever having written that.

EMILIE: But you implied it.

IBSEN: You seem to have studied my plays very thoroughly, Fraulein Bardach.

EMILIE: Of course. All of us have.

IBSEN: All of whom?

EMILIE: Everyone my age. Everyone who's young.

(*The dance music stops.*)

IBSEN: They've stopped dancing. Now we must go back.

EMILIE: They'll start again soon.

IBSEN: I think we should go back.

EMILIE: I want to go on talking to you.

IBSEN: But they will –

EMILIE: Oh, never mind *them.*

(*The dance music begins again.*)

IBSEN: What have you got there?

EMILIE: A rose.

IBSEN: You've been stealing.

EMILIE: Yes.

IBSEN: Do you often steal things?

EMILIE: I often want to.

IBSEN: Oh? What kind of things?

EMILIE: (*After a moment.*) Things other people have and I haven't.

IBSEN: You seem to be of a well-to-do family. There can't be much that other young ladies have and you haven't.

EMILIE: I didn't mean that.

IBSEN: What, then?

EMILIE: Never you mind.

IBSEN: But I do mind.

(*She fixes the rose in his buttonhole.*)

Why did you do that?

EMILIE: They'll think you stole it and not me.

IBSEN: I think I know what you steal. Or would like to steal.

EMILIE: Oh? What?

IBSEN: Men. Who belong to other women.

(*She does not answer.*)

Well, am I right?

EMILIE: Perhaps.

(*He clacks his tongue reprovingly.*)

I don't do it, though. It's only something I think about. It must be exciting to take. (*To herself.*) Or be –

IBSEN: Or what?

EMILIE: Nothing.

(*He stops walking and looks at her.*)

Oh, look! (*Points upwards.*) Isn't that beautiful?

IBSEN: What?

EMILIE: That spire. In the moonlight.

IBSEN: Yes, very pretty. I suppose that must be the town church.

EMILIE: I love spires. Spires and towers. And mountains. Anything high. Don't you?

IBSEN: No. They frighten me.

EMILIE: Frighten you?

IBSEN: I've always had a fear of heights. (*Pause.*) The first thing I remember is being up in a tower. My nurse had taken me up there – I can't have been more than two or three. I remember staring down at the people below, and I began to scream. I've always been afraid of towers ever since.

EMILIE: (*Staring up at the spire.*) I love them. They make me feel – dizzy.

IBSEN: And you like that feeling? Of being dizzy?

EMILIE: Oh, yes! It's as though I heard – a strange sound –

IBSEN: What kind of a sound?

EMILIE: (*Pause.*) I can't describe it. (*Pause.*) What else are you frightened of?

IBSEN: Many things.

EMILIE: What especially? (*He pauses a long time.*) Come on! Tell me!

IBSEN: Old age. And youth.

EMILIE: (*Amazed.*) Why youth?

IBSEN: I don't know.

EMILIE: But young people admire you so. You oughtn't to be afraid of us. We can't hurt you.

IBSEN: Perhaps not.

EMILIE: Then why?

IBSEN: (*Shortly.*) I tell you, I don't know.

EMILIE: It's silly to be frightened of something for no reason.

IBSEN: That is the worst kind of fear. The fear of the unknown.

(*Suddenly, impulsively, she takes his hand and kisses it. He turns to her. She looks at him.*)

FRAU BARDACH: (*Enter and peers around.*) Emilie!

(*EMILIE lets go of his hand and they turn.*)

Emilie! Is that you there? Where have you been? Who is that with you? (*Recognises IBSEN and changes her tone.*) Herr Ibsen! I beg your pardon! I hope my daughter has not been disturbing you?

IBSEN: Disturbing me? By no means.

FRAU BARDACH: I noticed she was not dancing, and was a little worried in case – but naturally, since she is with you – ! I hope she has not been asking too many questions?

IBSEN: We have been admiring the moonlight together.

EMILIE: And the roses.

FRAU BARDACH: Without a wrap! You'll catch cold.

(*EMILIE curtseys to him like a small girl. He bows formally. She takes her mother's arm; they return to the dance. The music swells louder. Black-out. When the lights go up, we see EMILIE in an armchair in a dressing-gown. She is writing in a diary.*)

EMILIE: Mamma was right. I caught a bad cold and had to spend several days in bed. Yesterday Ibsen came to see me. He remained with me a long while and was both kind and sympathetic. (*Pause.*) He came again today, at exactly the same time as yesterday. We talked a great deal together. He asked me endless questions, and seemed particularly keen to catch me in a lie.

IBSEN: (*Has walked over during this speech and is seated by her.*) Do you always wear pearls, even in bed?

EMILIE: Always. (*Pause.*) Ibsen has begun to talk to me quite seriously about myself. He stayed with me a long time on Saturday, and again this evening. Our being together cannot but have some painful influence over me. He puts such strong feeling into what he says to me. His words often give me a sensation of terror and cold. (*The lights change.*)

IBSEN: (*As Solness. Leans back in his chair, staring at her.*) Isn't it strange, Hilde? The more I think about it now – the more it seems to me as though for years I've been torturing myself trying to remember something – something – something that had happened to me and that I must have forgotten. But I could never understand what it was.

EMILIE: (*As Hilde Wangel.*) You ought to have tied a knot in your handkerchief, Master Builder.

IBSEN: (*As Solness.*) Then I'd only have gone round wondering what the knot stood for.
(*EMILIE laughs.*)
I'm glad you've come to me just at this time.

EMILIE: (*As Hilde. Looks into his eyes.*) Are you glad, Master Builder?

IBSEN: (*As Solness.*) I've been alone. Staring at it all, so helpless. (*Lowers his voice.*) You see – I've begun to be so afraid – so terribly afraid – of youth.

EMILIE: (*As Hilde. Scornfully.*) Youth? Is youth something to be afraid of?

IBSEN: (*As Solness.*) Yes, it is. That's why I've shut myself up. (*Secretively.*) Some day; youth will come to me and thunder on my door, and force its way in to me.

EMILIE: (*As Hilde.*) Then I think you ought to go out and open the door.

IBSEN: (*As Solness.*) Open the door?

EMILIE: (*As Hilde.*) Yes. And let youth in. As a friend.

IBSEN: No, no. Youth means retribution. It marches at the head of a rebel army. Under a new banner.

EMILIE: (*Looks at him.*) Can you use me, Master Builder?
(*The lights change back.*)
(*Diary.*) He talks about the most serious things in life, and believes in me so much. He expects from me much, much more than I am afraid he will ever find. Never in his whole life, he says, has he found so much joy in knowing anyone. He never admired anyone as he admires me.

IBSEN: (*Picks up a book from the table.*) What are you reading? (*Looks at the dust jacket.*) Still *Endymion?*

EMILIE: Take off the dust jacket.
(*He does. Looks at her reprovingly.*)

IBSEN: *The Comedy of Love.* Why this? (*Indicates the false dust jacket.*) Doesn't your mother approve of your reading my plays?

EMILIE: Not that one. She said it was very advanced.

IBSEN: I wrote it a long time ago. Nearly thirty years. Even my own theatre in Norway, where I was the director, rejected it.

EMILIE: Were you surprised?

IBSEN: Why do you ask that?

EMILIE: Mamma said she thought the theme rather wicked. It must have seemed even more so thirty years ago. (*Opens book and points to a passage.*) 'If you love someone, don't marry them. And if you want a happy marriage, beware of the person you love.'
(*He hands the book back to her. She takes it. For a moment their two hands are close, though not touching, as both hold the book.*).

IBSEN: You have beautiful hands.

EMILIE: Have I?

IBSEN: I once saw a very famous actress performing in one of my plays. She was terrible – terrible! Afterwards they brought her to my box and I had to say something to her. All I could think of was: 'You have beautiful hands.'

EMILIE: (*Laughs.*) Were they beautiful?

IBSEN: She knew how to use them.

EMILIE: Do you enjoy watching your plays?

IBSEN: I hate it. I never go unless I have to.

EMILIE: Why not?

IBSEN: They don't understand.

EMILIE: The actors or the critics?

IBSEN: Neither. Do you always wear pearls, even in bed?

EMILIE: You asked me that before. Yes, always. Why are you so shy?

IBSEN: Because I am ugly.

EMILIE: You aren't ugly.

IBSEN: I have always regarded myself as such.

EMILIE: I think you're beautiful. Sometimes, anyway.

IBSEN: Sometimes? When?

EMILIE: When you're angry.

IBSEN: When have you seen me angry?

EMILIE: When we first met. Up on the mountain. You suddenly looked at me in a way I'd never seen before. It was – terrible –

IBSEN: Terrible?

EMILIE: Yes. Frightfully exciting, though. (*Simply.*) That was when I fell in love with you.

IBSEN: That's a very childish thing to say.

EMILIE: Why?

IBSEN: I have nothing to offer you.

EMILIE: (*In a different voice.*) You can offer me what I want most.

IBSEN: (*Hypnotised by her as she is by him.*) What is that?

EMILIE: You could take me up on to a high mountain. And show me –

IBSEN: (*Slowly.*) All the glory of the world?

EMILIE: (*Whispers.*) Yes.

IBSEN: Is that what you want?

EMILIE: Yes. That's what I want.

IBSEN: And you think I could do that for you?

EMILIE: You know you could.

(*IBSEN Laughs.*)

Why are you laughing?

IBSEN: It's unthinkable.

EMILIE: Why?

IBSEN: For all sorts of reasons.

EMILIE: What reasons?

IBSEN: Firstly, I am married. Secondly, I am forty-three years older than you. Thirdly – (*Stops.*)

EMILIE: Thirdly – you're afraid?

IBSEN: Yes.

EMILIE: Of youth – and old age.

IBSEN: Not only that.

EMILIE: Of – the scandal?

IBSEN: Partly. And of other things too.

EMILIE: What other things?

IBSEN: Falling.

(*He gets up and walks over to the window.*)

EMILIE: But you're tempted. (*He turns his eyes on her.*) Admit it!

IBSEN: No, I am not tempted. (*Takes out his watch.*) And now I think we have talked long enough. My wife will be wondering where I am.

EMILIE: Come here. Come here.

IBSEN: (*Goes slowly towards her.*) Are you trying to hypnotise me, young lady?

EMILIE: Hypnotise? What's that?

IBSEN: Mesmerise.

EMILIE: Oh, that. Do you think I'm trying to send you to sleep?

IBSEN: I think you are trying to gain control over my mind.

EMILIE: (*Says nothing for a moment, then laughs.*) Well, I like that! I should say it was the other way about.

IBSEN: What do you mean?

EMILIE: I think it's you who have got control over my mind.

IBSEN: Don't be ridiculous. If I had control over your mind, you wouldn't be trying to persuade me to do something I don't want to do.

EMILIE: But you do want it.

IBSEN: I've told you –

EMILIE: Yes, you do. I'm not just saying what *I* want. I'm saying what *you* want. But what you're frightened to say yourself. That's true, isn't it?

IBSEN: Of course not.

EMILIE: Be honest now.

(*Pause.*)

IBSEN: It cannot be true.

EMILIE: (*The other voice speaks in her again.*) Mine is the voice you must listen to.

IBSEN: Yours is the voice I must not listen to. If you like. I have always been afraid of listening to that voice. And I don't intend to start now.

EMILIE: Some time you must. (*She fixes her eyes on his.*) Mine is the voice you have always longed to hear.

IBSEN: Yours is the voice I have always been afraid to hear.

EMILIE: Because you longed to hear it.

IBSEN: Perhaps. But –

EMILIE: You can't close your ears to it for ever.

IBSEN: I can try.

EMILIE: Look at me.

IBSEN: What is this power you have gained over me, Emilie?

EMILIE: Your own power. It is your voice that is saying these things, not mine.

(*She looks at him. Suddenly she becomes timid. Now their roles change, and the voice speaks in him instead of in her.*)

IBSEN: Suppose you were right –

EMILIE: Yes?

IBSEN: Suppose I did say: 'I will take you up on to a high mountain and show you all the glory of the world – ?'

EMILIE: Yes.

IBSEN: Would you come?

EMILIE: (*A little scared.*) Yes.

IBSEN: You realise the price you would have to pay?

EMILIE: I'm not afraid of scandal.

IBSEN: I didn't mean the scandal.

EMILIE: What, then?

IBSEN: I mean that, once you had seen all the glory of the world, you could never be content until you owned it. Until it was all yours.

EMILIE: I wouldn't be.

IBSEN: But suppose something happened that –

EMILIE: Yes?

IBSEN: That made it impossible for you to get it?

EMILIE: At least I would have seen it. (*Pause. The voice speaks in her again.*) You are the one I've been waiting for.

IBSEN: How did you come to be what you are, Emilie?

EMILIE: (*Whispers.*) How did you make me what I am?

IBSEN: You speak as though you were a character I created.

EMILIE: I am. You created me long ago.

IBSEN: Perhaps you are right. (*Gets up and walks over to the window.*) Long ago I met someone like you. I was twenty-three at the time; she was only fifteen. Rikke, her name was – short for Henrikke. That was before I met Suzannah, of course. We decided to marry. In a way, we did marry.

EMILIE: How do you mean, in a way?

IBSEN: There used to be an old custom in Norway. Two people who loved each other and couldn't afford to get married properly, or had no priest near them, would buy each other rings. And they would fasten these rings together, with a piece of string or perhaps a key chain, and they would throw these rings together into the sea. Then they would say that they had been married by the sea, and that would be as binding as any church wedding. Rikke and I did this. But then –

EMILIE: Go on.

IBSEN: Then her father found out about this. And he forbade it.

EMILIE: But what could he do? You were already married.

IBSEN: He said that if I continued to see her, he would see to it that I lost my job at the theatre. That I was driven out of town – and would never be able to get a job anywhere else. He was in a position to do that.

EMILIE: But you could have gone abroad with her?

IBSEN: No. She was too young. He could have stopped us.

EMILIE: You should have – (*Stops.*)

IBSEN: What?

EMILIE: You should have given her a child. Then he would have had to allow her to marry you.

IBSEN: I couldn't have done that, Emilie.

EMILIE: Why not?

IBSEN: Because I already had a child.

EMILIE: But I thought you said – Oh. I see.

IBSEN: It happened when I was eighteen. I was working as assistant to an apothecary in a little town called Grinstad. The apothecary had a servant-girl. She was ten years older than me. I didn't love her – we just – and she had a child. I was already paying for him. I couldn't have afforded to marry Rikke and lose my job – especially if her father had cut her off, as he would have done. Besides –

EMILIE: Besides – you were afraid of the scandal?

IBSEN: Yes.

EMILIE: So you gave up seeing her?

IBSEN: Yes.

EMILIE: And married Suzannah instead?

IBSEN: It was for the best. Without Suzannah, I would never have become what I am. She made me go on writing. She believed in me when no one else did – when I'd even given up believing in myself.

EMILIE: Did you never love her?

IBSEN: I knew that, if I was to succeed as a writer, she was the one I needed.

EMILIE: But now you have succeeded.

IBSEN: Yes.

EMILIE: Then now you can begin to live.

IBSEN: I have no right –

EMILIE: Haven't you said again and again that a person's first duty is to himself?

IBSEN: But Suzannah is old. I cannot leave her.

EMILIE: Other men have mistresses. You don't need to divorce her. You could just leave her for a year. Or six months even. You've been away from her before, haven't you?

IBSEN: Yes.

EMILIE: For months on end?

IBSEN: Yes. But alone.

THE SUMMER IN GOSSENSASS

EMILIE: She needn't know.

IBSEN: But your parents. They would never allow it.
And you are under age.

EMILIE: If I went, they wouldn't dare do anything.

IBSEN: Why not?

EMILIE: (*Smiles.*) Because of the scandal.

IBSEN: But there'd be one anyway.

EMILIE: Not for them. Nobody would know it was me who
was with you. I could use another name. There might be
for you, but why should you care? You're too big to need
to worry about that. Great men often have mistresses.
People accept it. I don't want to marry you, you know.
I only want a year with you. Just enough time to see –

IBSEN: All the glory of the world?

EMILIE: (*Whispers.*) Yes!

IBSEN: Emilie – !

(*FRAU BARDACH enters.*)

FRAU BARDACH: Well, Emilie, are you feeling better – ?
(*Sees IBSEN.*) Why, Herr Ibsen! Emilie, what an honour!

IBSEN: The honour has been mine, Frau Bardach.

FRAU BARDACH: Ah, nonsense! I do hope Emilie hasn't
been boring you with stupid questions. She is a little
childish sometimes, still.

IBSEN: Childish?

FRAU BARDACH: I sometimes wonder if she'll ever
grow up.
(*She looks fondly at EMILIE, who is lying back in her chair,
the enigmatic smile on her face. She begins to finger her
pearls.*)

EMILIE: (*Alone in her dressing-gown.*) Mamma has just
gone out, so that I have the room to myself. At last
I am free to put down the incredible things of these
recent days. How poor and insufficient are words! Tears
say these things better. Passion had come when it
cannot lead to anything, when both of us are bound by
so many ties. Eternal obstacles! Are they in my will?
Or are they in an outpouring like this? It could never
go so far, and yet – ! (*She takes off her dressing-gown and*

walks across in ordinary dress to join the others in the salon.)
The days we have still to spend can now be counted.
I don't think about the future. The present is too much.
When he talks to me as he does, I often feel that I must
go far away from here – far away! And yet I suffer at
the thought of leaving him. I suffer most from his
impatience, his restlessness. I begin to feel it now, even
when we are in the salon, quite apart from each other.
(*Pause.*) Last night, Baron A said he loved me. But how
much calmer *he* was, how articulate, beside this volcano,
so terribly beautiful!

SUZANNAH: (*Limps across on her way out and stops by
EMILIE.*) What a pretty dress!
(*EMILIE closes her diary and rises, embarrassed.*)
Blue suits you. I was never able to wear blue. Did you
get it in Vienna?

EMILIE: Yes.

SUZANNAH: And those shoes?

EMILIE: Yes.

SUZANNAH: (*Kindly.*) Charming. You have exquisite taste.

EMILIE: Thank you.
(*SUZANNAH smiles and limps out.*)
(*Perplexed.*) His wife shows me much attention.
(*The light fade. When they come up, EMILIE and FRAU
BARDACH are together. EMILIE has the pearls in her hands
and is staring at them; this is her private image. The pearls
glow in the light. A faint tapping on the window is heard.*)

FRAU BARDACH: What's that? Rain?

EMILIE: (*Looks out.*) No. Snow.

FRAU BARDACH: Already? What date is it?

EMILIE: The eighteenth of September.

FRAU BARDACH: I'd forgotten how early the winter
comes here. We shall have to leave.

EMILIE: Oh, no!

FRAU BARDACH: Once it's started to snow, the summer's
ended. There's no point staying after that. We'd better go
back to Vienna tomorrow.

EMILIE: Tomorrow! Oh, mother! A few days longer, please!

FRAU BARDACH: No, dear. Tomorrow.

EMILIE: (*Diary.*) Our last day at Gossensass! Then nothing but memory will remain. He says that tomorrow he will stand on the ruins of his happiness. These last two months are more important in his life than anything else that has gone before. He talked about his plans. I alone am in them – I, and I again. I feel quieter because he is quieter, though yesterday he was terrible.

SUZANNAH: (*To IBSEN, on far side of stage.*) It's beginning to snow.

IBSEN: Yes?

SUZANNAH: We shall have to leave.

IBSEN: There's no hurry. It may only be a shower. Anyway, it will be beautiful here with the snow.

SUZANNAH: We have no warm clothes here.

IBSEN: We could buy some.

SUZANNAH: These rooms are draughty already.
(*Pause.*)

IBSEN: I find them warm.

SUZANNAH: I think I shall go back to Munich at the weekend. (*Pause.*) You can stay if you want to.

IBSEN: (*After a pause.*) Of course not, Suzannah. I shall come with you.
(*She does not reply, but sits there, crocheting.*)

EMILIE: (*Alone.*) The obstacles! How they grow more numerous, the more I think of them! The difference of age – his wife – his son – all that there is to keep us apart! Did this have to happen? Could I have foreseen it? Could I have prevented it?
(*IBSEN, SUZANNAH, EMILIE and FRAU BARDACH move their chairs so as to suggest the hotel lounge, the IBSENS on one side, the BARDACHS on the other. Both SUZANNAH and FRAU BARDACH are crocheting. IBSEN and EMILIE are pretending to read, he a newspaper, she a book. She longs for him to come and speak to her. He is not reading any more than she is. His eyes come up and meet hers; then he drops them again. He rises and moves restlessly to the window.*)
Mother, why don't you go and say something to Frau Ibsen. I'm sure she'd like it.

FRAU BARDACH: I think I ought to wait for her to
approach me.

EMILIE: You know how shy she is. And it's our last day.

FRAU BARDACH: I never know what to talk to her about.
Oh, dear – perhaps you're right. I suppose it's my duty.
(*She goes over to SUZANNAH and sits down beside her.
IBSEN wanders across to EMILIE.*)

IBSEN: (*Bows formally.*) Good morning, Fraulein Bardach.

EMILIE: Good morning, Herr Ibsen.

IBSEN: (*Glances at the chair which FRAU BARDACH has
vacated.*) May I – ?

EMILIE: Of course.

IBSEN: (*Sits.*) So, tonight you are leaving.

EMILIE: Yes.

IBSEN: And we leave on Saturday. (*Pause.*) I am glad of
that. I should have hated to stay on here.

EMILIE: Would you?

IBSEN: This snow. Why did it have to come so early,
just this year?

EMILIE: When will I see you?

IBSEN: I don't know. I'll write.

EMILIE: (*Urgently.*) Soon!

IBSEN: (*Looks at her.*) Tell me, Emilie –

EMILIE: Yes?

IBSEN: You are quite sure that you want to do this?

EMILIE: Yes! Yes! (*Pause.*) When?

IBSEN: I can't say exactly when.

EMILIE: Why not?

IBSEN: There are things to be arranged. My wife – and my
son –

EMILIE: Have you become afraid again?

IBSEN: Again? I have always been afraid of this. Sometimes
I think it's impossible. Perhaps that is why it tempts me so
– beckons and tempts me.

EMILIE: Because it seems impossible?

IBSEN: Yes. Emilie – is it possible?

EMILIE: Of course! You know it is!
(*The two older women glance towards her. He makes a warning
gesture to her to lower her voice.*)

IBSEN: Is it possible? Or is it madness?

EMILIE: What if it is? Who wants always to be sane?

IBSEN: Does the thought of this never make you afraid?

EMILIE: Of course it does.

IBSEN: And yet you still want to – ?

EMILIE: Don't you see? That's what makes it so frightfully exciting. To do what one's afraid of! Haven't you ever done that?

IBSEN: No.

EMILIE: Well, you'll have to some time. It might as well be now.

(*She holds his eyes. Now she is the one who hypnotises.*)

That tiepin you're wearing –

IBSEN: Yes?

EMILIE: Is it real pearl?

IBSEN: Yes.

EMILIE: Let me hold it. Just for a moment. (*He removes it silently and gives it to her. She stares at it in her hands.*) Beautiful – beautiful!

IBSEN: Why are you so obsessed with pearls?

EMILIE: (*Not hearing him.*) Beautiful! It's like a human eye! (*Suddenly gives a small happy laugh and hands it back to him.*) Here. Now you can put it back again. (*Pause. A little frightened.*) Why are you looking at me like that? (*He stares at her. Suddenly he seems immense and she small and scared. She whispers.*) Stop it! (*Gives a small, excited laugh.*) Here, take your pin.

IBSEN: (*His face becomes mild and expressionless again. He takes the pin and fastens it primly into his tie.*) Thank you. And now I must return to my wife.

EMILIE: (*Urgently.*) Will I see you again before I go?

IBSEN: I hardly think it will be possible for us to meet alone.

EMILIE: I *must* see you alone.

IBSEN: No. (*Glances at the old women.*) If your mother should suspect –

EMILIE: But I *must* – !

IBSEN: (*Firmly.*) No.

EMILIE: But you won't change your mind! Promise!
IBSEN: (*After a moment.*) I promise.
EMILIE: You'll take me up on to a high mountain –
IBSEN: Yes.
EMILIE: And show me – ! Come on! Say it!
(*A long pause.*)
IBSEN: All the glory of the world.
(*FRAU BARDACH rises and walks over towards them.*)
EMILIE: You promise?
FRAU BARDACH: Herr Ibsen, your wife and I have been having such an interesting conversation. What a delightful and impressive lady she is. She is worthy of you, indeed.
IBSEN: Thank you. (*Turns to go.*)
EMILIE: Herr Ibsen!
IBSEN: Yes?
EMILIE: Will you write something in my album?
(*Takes it from her handbag and holds it out to him. IBSEN hesitates.*)
FRAU BARDACH: Please, Herr Ibsen! Something for her to show her friends when we return to Vienna.
IBSEN: (*Stiffly.*) Of course. (*Takes the album, sits at the table, reflects, then writes briefly. He rises and hands it back to EMILIE.*) I probably won't be seeing you again before you leave, so may I wish you both a pleasant journey? (*Bows formally.*)
FRAU BARDACH: Thank you! Thank you, Herr Ibsen!
(*IBSEN and EMILIE look at each other for a moment. Then he turns and walks back to SUZANNAH. EMILIE looks at her album.*)
What has Herr Ibsen written in your album, Emilie?
EMILIE: A line from Goethe's Faust.
FRAU BARDACH: What does it say?
EMILIE: 'Oh, high and painful joy – to struggle for the unobtainable!'
SUZANNAH: (*On far side of stage, to IBSEN.*) The snow seems heavier tonight.
IBSEN: Yes.
(*EMILIE takes out her diary, unclasps it and begins to write.*)

FRAU BARDACH: (*Fondly.*) Still keeping your diary, Emilie?

EMILIE: Yes.

FRAU BARDACH: That's good. It'll be nice to read it during the winter, and remind yourself of this holiday.

EMILIE: Yes.

(*FRAU BARDACH buries herself again in her newspaper. EMILIE faces downstage and speaks the words she has written.*)

He means to possess me. That is his absolute will. He intends to overcome all obstacles. I listen as he describes what is to lie before us – going from one country to another – I with him – enjoying his triumphs together. Our parting was easier than I had feared.

(*The lights fade.*

Lights up. IBSEN's house in Munich on one side of the stage, EMILIE's in Vienna on the other. IBSEN at his desk, writing. EMILIE is reading his letter.)

IBSEN: (*Writing.*) Munich, 7th October 1889. With my whole heart I thank you, beloved Fräulein, for the dear and delightful letter which I received on the last day of my stay in Gossensass, and have read over and over again.

(*She smiles and kisses the letter.*)

There the last autumn day was a very sad one, or it was so to me. No more sunshine. Everything – gone. I went to walk in the Pflerschtal. There is a bench where two can commune together.

(*She raises her eyes from the letter, remembering.*)

But the bench was empty and I went by without sitting down. So, too, the big salon was waste and desolate. Do you remember the big, deep bay-window on the right from the verandah? Smelling so sweetly – but how empty! – how lonely! – how forsaken! – We are back here at home in Munich – and you in Vienna. You write that you feel surer of yourself, more independent, happier.

(*She looks sad; the words are not true.*)

A new play begins to dawn in me. I want to work on it
this winter, transmuting into it the glowing inspiration
of the summer. But the end may be a disappointment.
I feel it. It is my way. I told you once that I only
correspond by telegraph. So take this letter as it is.
You will know what it means. A thousand greetings
from your devoted H. I.

EMILIE: (*Puts down letter.*) Today at last came Ibsen's
long-expected letter. He wants me to read between the
lines. But do not the lines themselves say enough? This
evening I paid Grandmamma a quite unpleasant visit.
The weather is hot and stuffy and so is Pappa's mood.
In other days this would have depressed me. But now – !

IBSEN: 15th October 1889. I received your letter with a
thousand thanks, and I have read it, and read it again.
Here I sit as usual at my desk, and would gladly work,
but cannot do so. My imagination is ragingly alive, but
is always straying to where in working hours it should
not. I cannot keep down the memories of the summer,
nor do I wish to. The things we have lived through I live
again and again – and still again. To make of them a
poem for the time being impossible. For the time being?
Shall I ever succeed in the future?
(*He looks at the sheet of paper on which he has been writing.
Gets up, walks over to the lamp and lights it. Reads to himself
from what he has written – his notes for the new play, but he
cannot move forward from them.*)
(*Reads.*) Hedda Gabler. Hedda is typical of people in her
position and with her character. One marries one person,
but one titillates one's imagination with another. One
leans back in one's chair, closes one's eyes and pictures
to oneself these adventures... But one lacks the courage
to partake actively. (*He puts the notes down and turns
towards EMILIE on her side of the room; now this is his letter
to her, but he speaks it to her.*) Do you remember that once
we talked about Folly and Madness – and you took up
the role of teacher, and remarked in your soft, musical
voice, and with your far-away look, that there is always a

difference between Folly and Madness? Well, then, I keep thinking over and over again – was it Folly or was it Madness that we should have come together? Or was it both Folly and Madness? Or was it neither? I believe the last is the only supposition that would stand the test. It was a simple necessity of nature. It was, equally, our fate...

EMILIE: I left Ibsen's letter unopened till I had finished everything and could read it quietly. But I was not quiet after reading it.

IBSEN: (*Reads his notes for the play again; to himself.*) Women...aren't all created to be mothers. They all crave sensuality, but are afraid of the scandal. (*He looks up, guiltily; it is his fear too.*) They know that life holds a purpose for them, but they cannot find that purpose. The great tragedy of life is that so many people have nothing to do but yearn for happiness without ever being able to find it.

EMILIE: Why does he not tell me of something to read instead of writing in a way to inflame my already excited imagination?

IBSEN: But to be an object of ridicule! Of ridicule! (*HELENE RAFF enters, young and attractive. She does not yet belong to either room.*) Who are you?

HELENE: Don't you remember?

IBSEN: Your face is familiar. I should remember –

HELENE: You didn't really notice me. I was staying at the hotel at Gossensass too. But you only had eyes for her. My name is Helene – Helene Raff. (*Comes downstage and speaks to the audience.*) I am a painter, and on my return to Munich I spent several days walking up and down Maximilian-strasse, where Ibsen lives, in the hope of seeing him. At last I was successful. He seemed not unpleased to see me.
(*Turns and smiles at him. He smiles back.*)
Next morning, I ran into him at an art exhibition. Later that day, we saw each other again. (*He comes up close behind her.*) Five days later he invited me to his apartment, where

I spent an hour with him. I found this very interesting but...upsetting. He spoke much about hypnosis and the power of the will.

IBSEN: The tragedy with you women is that your will tends to remain undeveloped. You dream and wait for something unknown that will give your lives meaning. As a result, your emotional lives are unhealthy, and you fall victims to disappointment.

EMILIE: *Our* lives are unhealthy! Only ours?

HELENE: When I left, he accompanied me down to the courtyard, and there he kissed me.

IBSEN: 29th October – Dear Fraulein Bardach. I have been meaning every day to write you a few words. So you leave my letters unopened until you are alone and quite undisturbed! (*Smiles.*) Don't be uneasy because just now I cannot work. In the back of my mind I am working all the time. I am dreaming over something which, when it has ripened, will become a play.

(*EMILIE smiles happily and turns the letter to read it again.*)
(*To himself.*) You women dream and wait for something unknown that will give your lives meaning. One marries Tessman, but one titillates one's fancy with Ejlert Lövborg. One leans back in one's chair, closes one's eyes and imagines his...adventures.

(*The lights change. HEDDA GABLER and EJLERT LÖVBORG; she on a sofa, he on a chair beside her.*)

LÖVBORG: Do you remember, Hedda, how I used to come up to your father's house in the afternoon – and the General sat by the window and read his newspapers – with his back towards us?

HEDDA: And we sat on the sofa in the corner –

LÖVBORG: Always reading the same illustrated magazines –

HEDDA: We hadn't any photograph album.

LÖVBORG: I regarded you as a kind of confessor. Told you things about myself which no one else knew about. What power did you have to make me confess such things?

HEDDA: You think I had some power over you?

LÖVBORG: All those oblique questions you asked. That you could sit there and ask me then, so unashamedly –

EMILIE: I? It was you who asked me.

IBSEN: It was you.

EMILIE: What are you trying to make of me?

IBSEN: You are what I choose to make of you.

LÖVBORG: Oh, why didn't you do it, Hedda? Why didn't you shoot me dead? As you threatened to?

HEDDA: I was afraid. Of the scandal.

EMILIE: *I* wasn't afraid –

LÖVBORG: Yes, Hedda. You're a coward at heart.

HEDDA: A dreadful coward.

(*The lighting changes back. IBSEN smiles, rises and goes towards HELENE.*)

EMILIE: (*Cries.*) *I* a coward – !

HELENE: On November 8th I visited Ibsen again.

(*She smiles at him, and he at her.*)

He was pleased at my coming. Three days later, I met him again. He wants to visit me. He accompanied me home. Tender parting. I asked him why he liked me and what he saw in me.

IBSEN: (*To HELEN.*) You are youth. And I need that. For my work, my writing.

HELENE: I was troubled that he had used certain phrases which reminded me of what Fraulein Bardach had told me at Gossensass. I asked him not to speak to me as he had done to her.

IBSEN: Oh, that was in the country. In town, one is more in earnest.

(*He goes to his desk. EMILIE sits, away from them, observing them both.*)

6th December 1889 – Dear Fraulein Bardach. How vividly your dear serene features remain with me in my memory! The same enigmatic princess stands behind them. In my imagination I always see you wearing the pearls which you love so much.

(*The harp theme again.*)

In this taste for pearls, I see something deeper, something hidden. I often think of it. Sometimes I think I have found the interpretation – and sometimes not.

(*EMILIE clasps the letter to her heart and closes her eyes.*)

22nd December. I read your letter over and over, for through it the voice of the summer awakens so clearly. I see – I experience again – the things we have lived together. As a lovely creature of the summer, dear Princess, I have known you, as a being of the season of butterflies and wild flowers. How I should like to see you as you are in winter! I am always with you in spirit!

EMILIE: Oh, the terror and beauty of having him care about me as he never cared about anyone else! But when he is suffering, he calls it 'high and painful joy'!

IBSEN: I see you in the Ring Strasse, light, quick, poised like a bird, gracious in velvet and furs. In *soirées*, in society, I also see you, and especially at the theatre, leaning back, a tired look in your mysterious eyes. I should like, too, to see you at home, but here I don't succeed, as I haven't the data. You have told me so little of your home-life – hardly anything definite. As a matter of fact, dear Princess, in many important details we are strangers to one another.

SUZANNAH: (*Enters with her stick, carrying a large envelope.*) A package has come for you.

IBSEN: (*At his desk, preoccupied.*) Open it for me, will you?

SUZANNAH: It's from Vienna.

(*Pause.*)

IBSEN: Leave it on the table, please.

(*She does so and goes. He gets up, walks over and opens the package. Takes out a photograph of EMILIE; no letter with it. He turns it over.*)

IBSEN: (*Reads.*) How much longer…?

EMILIE: How much longer are you going to make me wait?

(*He looks at this for some moments, then turns the photograph over again and looks at the face. We hear again, faintly, the waltz that was playing when they stood in the rose-garden.*)

SUZANNAH: (*Enters.*) Are you ready for lunch?

(*He does not reply but continues to stare at the photograph.*)

What are you looking at?

IBSEN: A photograph.

SUZANNAH: (*Without malice.*) Ah – Fraulein Bardach?

IBSEN: Yes.

> (*She notices the inscription on the back as he looks at it. She reads it but does not react.*)

SUZANNAH: May I see it?

IBSEN: Of course. (*Hands it to her.*)

SUZANNAH: (*Looks at it.*) Yes, she's a pretty child. How old did she say she was?

IBSEN: Eighteen, I think.

SUZANNAH: (*Glances at the desk.*) You haven't written anything this morning?

IBSEN: No. I have been thinking.

SUZANNAH: Well, shall I ask the maid to serve lunch?

IBSEN: Yes.

SUZANNAH: Very well.

> (*She limps out. IBSEN stands holding the photograph. Suddenly he puts his hand to his forehead and closes his eyes, as though dizzy. Back-projected, we see his body falling through space. He remains thus for some moments, then opens his eyes.*)

EMILIE: (*Whispers.*) You're not old!

IBSEN: Yes, I am old.

EMILIE: You're young!

> (*SUZANNAH limps in through the door.*)

You'll always be young.

> (*His eyes glow as he seems to obey the voice. Then he puts his hand again to his eyes and closes them. We see the falling image again.*)

SUZANNAH: Well, Ibsen. Are you ready?

> (*Pause*)

IBSEN: Yes, Suzannah. I'm ready now.

> (*Some brief, back-projected stills to suggest the passing of days. IBSEN walking out of doors, his hands clasped behind his back, top-hatted and formidable – actual photographs of him.*)

HELENE: (*As these stills are shown.*) Ibsen's son Sigurd once wrote: I believe that if Mother had not compelled Father to sit down at his desk every morning, half of his work might never have been written. No doubt there were times when he revolted against her strong will and wished himself far away so that he could submerge himself in his daydreams. But if he had lost her for good he would have been inconsolable. If she had withdrawn her will, he would have been lost indeed. He was the genius, she was the character – his character – and well he knew it.

(*The post clatters through EMILIE's letter-box. She runs to the door but finds no letters for her. The lighting changes. She puts her hands to her head; he is possessing her again. HEDDA and LÖVBORG continue their scene from when we last saw them, she on the sofa, he on a chair close to her.*)

LÖVBORG: Tell me one thing, Hedda. Didn't you love me? Not – just a little?

HEDDA: (*Hard and cynical.*) Well, now, Ejlert, I wonder. No, I think we were just good friends. Really good friends, who could tell each other everything. (*Smiles.*) You certainly poured out your heart to me.

LÖVBORG: You begged me to.

HEDDA: Looking back on it, there was something beautiful and fascinating – and brave – about the way we told each other everything. That secret friendship no-one else knew about.

LÖVBORG: Yes, I regarded you as a kind of confessor. Told you things about myself which no-one else knew about. Oh, what power did you have to make me confess such things?

HEDDA: Power?

LÖVBORG: That you could sit there and ask me such questions. So unashamedly –

EMILIE: Ibsen, it was *you* who asked *me* – !

LÖVBORG: So unashamedly, Hedda.

HEDDA: You answered willingly enough.

LÖVBORG: You didn't love me then, Hedda. You just wanted – knowledge. But if that was so, why did you break it off?

HEDDA: That was your fault, Ejlert.

LÖVBORG: It was you who put an end to it.

HEDDA: Yes, when I realised that our friendship was threatening to develop into something else.

LÖVBORG: Oh, why didn't you *do* it?

HEDDA: I was afraid. Of the scandal.

LÖVBORG: Yes, Hedda. You're a coward at heart.

HEDDA: A dreadful coward. Luckily for you.

(*The lighting changes back.*)

EMILIE: This isn't me you're portraying! It's you, in skirts!

IBSEN: Don't be so ridiculous!

EMILIE: Say her lines, and see if they don't fit you like a glove.

IBSEN: Now you are being hysterical.

EMILIE: Dare you say her lines?

IBSEN: Of course I *dare*. But –

EMILIE: Very well.

(*They take the places of the others. She speaks from LÖVBORG's chair.*)

Tell me one thing. Didn't you love me? Not – just a little?

IBSEN: (*Speaking HEDDA's lines.*) Well now, I wonder. No, I think we were just good friends, who could tell each other everything. (*Smiles.*) You certainly poured out your heart to me.

EMILIE: You begged me to.

IBSEN/HEDDA: Looking back on it, there was something beautiful and fascinating – and brave – the way we told each other everything. That secret friendship no-one else knew about.

EMILIE/LÖVBORG: Yes. I regarded you as a kind of confessor. Told you things about myself which no-one else knew about. Oh, what power did you have to make me confess such things?

IBSEN: Power? (*Now he is completely on the defensive.*)

EMILIE: That you could sit there and ask me such questions. So unashamedly –

IBSEN: You answered willingly enough.

EMILIE: You didn't love me, then. You just wanted knowledge. But is that was so, why did you break it off?

IBSEN: (*Vehemently, defensively.*) That was your fault!

EMILIE: It was you who put an end to it.

IBSEN: (*Hesitates long before saying this line.*) Yes, when I realized that our friendship was threatening to develop into something. Something else.

EMILIE: Oh, Hedda, why didn't you do it?

IBSEN: I was afraid of the scandal.

EMILIE: Yes. You're a coward at heart.

IBSEN: A dreadful coward. Luckily for you.
(*Pause.*)

EMILIE: (*As herself.*) Well, Ibsen? Whom does the cap fit? (*No reply. Bitterly.*) Portrait of the Dramatist as a Young Woman!
(*She returns to her room and sits. He sits at his desk, in lamplight. Slowly his hand goes out and takes a sheet of notepaper. He begins to write.*)

IBSEN: February 6th 1890. Long, very long, have I left your last, dear letter – read and read again – without an answer. Take today my heartfelt thanks for it, though given in very few words. (*Pause.*) Henceforth, till we see each other again, you will hear very little from me, and very seldom. Believe me, it is better so. It is the only right thing. It is a matter of conscience – (*Pause.*) It is a matter of conscience with me to end this correspondence, or at least to limit it. You yourself should have as little to do with me as possible. With your young life, you have other aims to follow, other tasks to fulfil. And I – I have told you so – can never be content with a mere exchange of letters. For me it is only half the thing. It is a false situation. Not to give myself wholly and unreservedly makes me unhappy. (*Pause. He is lying and knows it.*) It is my nature. I cannot change it. You are so delicately subtle, so instinctively penetrating, that you will easily see what I mean. When we are together again, you will be in my thoughts. You will be even more so when we no longer have to stop at this wearisome halfway-house or correspondence. A thousand greetings. Your H.I.

EMILIE: (*Puts down the letter; abstractedly picks up her pearls and stares at them as into a pool.*) What is my inner life after Ibsen's letter? Henceforth I will be silent, silent... Will he never write to me any more? I cannot think about it. Who could? And yet, not to do so is in his nature. In his very kindness there is often cruelty.

(*Christmas bells. Carol singing outside. SUZANNAH brings in to IBSEN, working at his desk, a pile of letters. He glances through them indifferently, not bothering to open them; comes across a small package; looks at the handwriting; pauses. Pushes it aside among the other unopened things and continues looking through the rest. After some seconds, half-unwillingly, he puts them down and takes up the package; looks at it; takes his scissors and cuts the string deliberately; puts scissors back on the desk; takes up his penknife and with the same deliberation slits the paper and opens it. Inside is something carefully wrapped in tissue. He unwraps it. It is a small Tyrolean cowbell with a childish painting on it. He looks at it. The waltz theme is repeated.*)

SUZANNAH: (*Who has been watching.*) What a pretty bell.

IBSEN: Yes, isn't it?

SUZANNAH: (*Picks it up and looks at it through her lorgnette.*) Very pretty. (*Tinkles it.*) Is this from Fraulein Bardach?

IBSEN: Yes.

SUZANNAH: Charming. How sweet of her to remember us. (*Goes.*)

(*IBSEN stares at the bell. It disturbs him. The waltz theme continues. He reaches for notepaper and writes.*)

IBSEN: I have duly received your letter, as well as the bell with the beautiful picture. I thank you for them, straight from the heart. My wife finds the picture –

EMILIE: (*Reading it.*) – very pretty. But I beg you, for the time being, not to write to me again. When conditions have changed, I will let you know. I shall soon send you my new play. Accept it in friendship – but in silence. How I should love to see you and talk with you again! Your always devoted H.I.

(*IBSEN blots the letter, puts it in an envelope, seals and stamps it. Picks up his usual handbell and is about to ring it;*

*puts it down and, after a moment, rinds EMILIE's bell
instead. The maid, LINA, enters.)*

LINA: You rang, sir?

IBSEN: Take this letter to the post, Lina.

LINA: But there's no post till Thursday, sir. It's Christmas
Eve –

IBSEN: I know. Take it all the same, will you?

LINA: Very good, sir.

IBSEN: *(As she turns to go.)* Oh, Lina.

LINA: Yes, sir?

IBSEN: Would your little daughter like this for Christmas?
(Hands her the bell.)

LINA: Oh, thank you, sir. *(Curtseys.)* It's beautiful!
*(She goes out with the bell. IBSEN remains motionless for a
moment, then reaches out for a large sheet of folio and, after
a few seconds, begins to write.)*

EMILIE: *(Throughout this speech of hers, IBSEN is writing or
pacing his room, composing.)* Dear Ibsen – please forgive me
for writing again so soon. I certainly do not wish you to
write to me frequently, and since you wish it, I shall also
refrain. What I have so often told you remains unaltered,
and I can never forget it. But can friendship bear not to
know if the other is ill or well, happy or wretched? And
if you do not write, how am I to know where we can find
each other again? Well, I'll be very, very patient. I can
wait. With love, Emilie.

IBSEN: *(To a Gentleman Friend.)* Do you know, my next
play is already hovering before me. Its general outline,
of course.

FRIEND: May I know what it's about?

IBSEN: I don't see it clearly yet. Only the outline. *(Drinks.)*
And the chief character.

FRIEND: Who is he?

IBSEN: It's a woman. A young woman I once met. Very
interesting. Very interesting. *(Drinks.)*

FRIEND: Tell me about her.

IBSEN: A remarkable character. She made me her
confidante. *(Drinks again.)* She told me she wasn't
interested in the idea of getting married. Said most likely

she'd never marry. What attracted her was to lure other women's husbands away from them.

FRIEND: You make her sound like a little demon.

IBSEN: She was like a bird of prey.

FRIEND: Did she try to include you among her victims?

IBSEN: (*Smiles.*) She tried. But she didn't get a hold of me. But I got hold of her. For my play.

FRIEND: That must have broken her heart.

IBSEN: Oh, I expect she managed to console herself with someone else. (*Drinks.*)

(*A package clatters through EMILIE's letter-box. She unwraps it. It is a book.*)

EMILIE: (*Reads the title.*) The Master Builder. (*Looks for a note. Sadly.*) No letter. (*She begins to read.*)

(*Lighting changes. EMILIE walks over towards IBSEN and stands facing him, hands on hips, hard and confident, as Hilde Wangel.*)

(*As Hilde.*) Master Builder?

IBSEN: (*As Solness. Turns to her.*) Yes, Hilde?

EMILIE: (*As Hilde.*) Have you a bad memory?

IBSEN: (*As Solness.*) A bad memory? Not that I'm aware of.

EMILIE: (*As Hilde.*) You took me in your arms and kissed me, Master Builder.

IBSEN: (*As Solness.*) I did?

EMILIE: (*As Hilde.*) Yes, you did. You took me in both your arms and bent me backwards and kissed me. Many, many times.

IBSEN: (*As Solness.*) Oh, but my dear, good Miss Wangel –

EMILIE: (*As Hilde.*) You're not going to deny it?

IBSEN: (*As Solness.*) I certainly am!

EMILIE: (*As Hilde. Looks at him scornfully.*) Oh, I see. (*She turns and walks slowly away, then stands motionless with her back towards him and her hands behind her. Short pause.*)

IBSEN: (*As Solness. Goes diffidently up behind her.*) Miss Wangel – !

(*She remains silent and motionless.*)

Don't stand there like a statue. All this that you've told me must be something you've dreamed. (*Touches her arm.*) Now, listen – !

(*She makes an impatient gesture with her arm.*)

(*A thought strikes him.*) Or – wait a moment! No, there's more to it than that.

(*She does not move.*)

(*He speaks softly but with emphasis.*) I must have thought all this. I must have wanted it – wished it – desired it. So that – ! Couldn't that be an explanation?

(*She remains silent.*)

(*He bursts out impatiently.*) Oh, damn it! Have it your own way – say I did it!

EMILIE: (*As Hilde. Turns her head slightly but does not look at him.*) You confess?

IBSEN: (*As Solness.*) Yes. Anything you say.

EMILIE: (*As Hilde.*) That you put your arms around me?

IBSEN: (*As Solness.*) Yes. Yes.

EMILIE: (*As Hilde.*) And bent me over backwards?

IBSEN: (*As Solness.*) Yes. Right back.

EMILIE: (*As Hilde.*) And kissed me?

IBSEN: (*As Solness.*) Yes. I kissed you.

EMILIE: (*As Hilde.*) Many times?

IBSEN: (*As Solness.*) As many as you like.

EMILIE: (*As Hilde. Turns quickly towards him, her eyes again glowing and excited.*) You see! I wormed it out of you in the end! (*As EMILIE.*) You did kiss me, you did!

IBSEN: (*As Solness. Ignoring this.*) Oh, there are so many invisible demons in the world, Hilde! Good demons and evil demons. Fair demons and dark. If only one always knew whether it was the fair that had hold of one, or the dark! (*Laughs.*) It would all be so simple.

EMILIE: (*As Hilde. Hard and excited.*) Or if only one had a really brash and hearty conscience! So that one dared to do what one wanted.

IBSEN: (*As Solness. Looks at her thoughtfully.*) Oh, I think most people are as cowardly as I, in that respect. (*Pause.*) The sagas tell about Vikings, who sailed to foreign lands, and plundered and burned and killed –

EMILIE: (*As Hilde.*) And carried away women –

IBSEN: (*As Solness.*) And kept them.

EMILIE: (*As Hilde.*) Took them home with them in their
ships –

IBSEN: (*As Solness.*) And used them like – like the worst
kind of trolls.

EMILIE: (*As Hilde. To herself, her eyes half-closed.*) I think that
must be so exciting!

IBSEN: (*As Solness. With a short, gruff laugh.*) To take a
woman, you mean?

EMILIE: (*As Hilde.*) To be taken.

IBSEN: (*As Solness. Looks at her for a moment.*) I see.

EMILIE: (*As Hilde.*) I can understand the women frightfully
well.

IBSEN: (*As Solness.*) Ah! Perhaps you would do the same
yourself?

EMILIE: (*As Hilde.*) Why not?

IBSEN: (*As Solness.*) Live – willingly – with a brute like that?

EMILIE: (*As Hilde.*) If he was a brute I'd come to grow
really fond –

IBSEN: (*As Solness.*) Could you grow fond of a man like that?

EMILIE: (*As Hilde.*) Oh, God, one can't help whom one
grows fond of, can one?

IBSEN: (*As Solness. Looks at her thoughtfully again.*) No, no –
I suppose it's the troll in us that decided that.

EMILIE: (*As Hilde. With a little laugh.*) And all those
blessed demons you know so much about. The fair and
the dark.

IBSEN: (*As Solness. Warmly, quietly.*) I hope the demons
choose kindly for you, Hilde.

EMILIE: (*As Hilde.*) They have chosen for me. Once and
for all.

IBSEN: (*As Solness. Looks deep into her eyes.*) Hilde – you are
like a new dawn. When I look at you, it is as though
I were watching the sunrise.

(*EMILIE becomes herself and almost breaks down.*)

IBSEN: (*As Solness. Sternly.*) Hilde!

EMILIE: (*As Hilde again.*) Tell me, Master Builder. Are you
sure you've never called to me? Silently?

IBSEN: (*As Solness. Quietly.*) I think I must have done.

EMILIE: (*As Hilde.*) What do you want from me?

IBSEN: (*As Solness.*) Your youth, Hilde.

EMILIE: (*As Hilde. Smiles.*) Youth, which you are so frightened of?

IBSEN: (*As Solness.*) And which in my heart I long for. (*Looks deep into her eyes.*) Hilde – you are like a wild bird of the forest.

EMILIE: (*As Hilde.*) Far from it. I'm not shy.

IBSEN: (*As Solness.*) No, no. There's more of the falcon in you.

EMILIE: (*As Hilde.*) Yes, perhaps. (*Violently.*) And why not a falcon? Why shouldn't I go hunting too? Get the prey I want? If only I can get my claws into it? Bring it to the ground! (*EMILIE as herself whispers.*) What are you making of me? I never said those things! I'm not like that!

IBSEN: (*As Solness. Sternly.*) Hilde! Do you know what you are?

EMILIE: (*Not yet Hilde again, whispers.*) A falcon, you said.

IBSEN: (*As Solness.*) No. You are like a new dawn. When I look at you, it is as though I were watching the sunrise.

EMILIE: (*She is Hilde now.*) Tell me, Master Builder – are you sure you've never called to me? Silently?

IBSEN: (*As Solness. Quietly.*) I think I must have done.

EMILIE: (*As Hilde.*) What do you want from me?

IBSEN: (*As Solness.*) Your youth, Hilde.

EMILIE: (*As Hilde. Smiles.*) Youth, which you are so frightened of?

IBSEN: (*As Solness.*) And which, in my heart, I long for. But it's no good, Hilde. Sooner or later, retribution will come.

EMILIE: (*As Hilde. Frightened, puts her hands over her ears.*) Don't talk like that! Do you want to take away from me what I value more than my life?

IBSEN: (*As Solness.*) And what's that?

EMILIE: (*As Hilde.*) To see you with a wreath in your hand, high, high up on a church tower!

IBSEN: (*As Solness.*) I've told you, I have no head for heights.

EMILIE: (*As Hilde.*) You said you'd make me a princess, and that you'd give me a kingdom. I want my kingdom, Master Builder!

IBSEN: (*As Solness.*) I begin to think that there is nothing in me that is safe from you, Hilde.

EMILIE: (*As Hilde. With half-closed eyes, whispers to herself.*) Frightfully exciting!
(*The lights change. She becomes EMILIE again.*) That's not the way it was! What are you doing to me? I wasn't like that! I'm not like that!

IBSEN: You are what I make you.

EMILIE: Was that all you wanted me for? As a model?
(*IBSEN does not reply.*)
You offered to show me all the glory of the world. Don't you think *I* could have shown some of it to *you*?

IBSEN: Keep out of my life.

EMILIE: (*Quietly.*) You're cowardly and cruel. That's a terrible price to pay for greatness.

IBSEN: It was the price I had to pay.

EMILIE: You didn't have to pay it.

IBSEN: (*Very hard.*) Are you suggesting that your happiness is more important to the world than my work?

EMILIE: To me, it is.

IBSEN: Not to anyone else.

HELENE: Ibsen's verdict on Emilie's character was generally accepted, and Emilie Bardach went down to history while she was still a young woman as a predatory little monster like Hilde Wangel. The mood of every play that Ibsen wrote after his meeting with Emilie is one of restrained and balked individuality. He had suppressed his emotional life for so long; now at last he had the opportunity to fulfil it, but was too timid – or too something – to do anything about it. As a result of his meeting with Emilie, a new glory, but also a new darkness, entered into his work.
(*The lights change.*)

EMILIE: (*Now she is an older woman.*) Borkman!

IBSEN: (*As Borkman.*) Ella!

133

EMILIE: (*As Ella.*) The Bible speaks of a mysterious sin for which there is no forgiveness. I've never understood what that meant before. Now I understand. The sin for which there is no forgiveness is to murder love in a human being.

IBSEN: (*As Borkman.*) And you say I have done that?

EMILIE: (*As Ella.*) You have.

IBSEN: (*As Borkman. Cold and controlled.*) It is only natural for you to see it like that. You are a woman. Consequently, nothing else in the whole world matters to you. You can only think about this one thing.

EMILIE: (*As Ella.*) Only that! Only that!

IBSEN: But you must remember that I am a man. As a woman you were, to me, the most precious thing in the world. But if need be (*Glances towards HELENE.*) – one woman can be replaced by another.

EMILIE: (*As Ella.*) You betrayed the woman you loved – me, me, me! You are guilty of double murder. The murder of your own soul, and mine.
(*She walks back to her chair and sits in it, very alone. The lights change to normal; then back again.*)

IBSEN: (*Equally alone, and suddenly very old.*) But listen how I have portrayed myself. In the foreground, beside a spring, there sits a man weighed down by guilt. I call him remorse – remorse for a forfeited life. He sits there, dipping his fingers in the rippling water, to wash them clean. And he is gnawed and tormented by the knowledge that he will never, never succeed. He will never, in all eternity, free himself and be granted resurrection. He must stay forever in his hell.
(*The lights change to normal.*)

HELENE: For seven years there was no contact between Ibsen and Emilie. Then, on his seventieth birthday, an occasion of great international celebration – for he was, with Tolstoy, the most famous writer in the world – she sent him a telegram of congratulation. His short letter of reply was the last communication between them.

IBSEN: (*At his desk.*) Christiana, 13th March 1898. Herzlich liebes Fraulein! Accept my most deeply felt thanks for you message. (*Pause.*) The summer in Gossensass was the happiest, the most beautiful, in my whole life. I scarcely dare to think of – and yet I must think of it, always. Always!

HELENE: Emilie Bardach died a spinster in 1955, aged 83 years.

(*Two huge photographs are back-projected of IBSEN and EMILIE as they looked when they met in Gossensass, he white-whiskered and titanic, she virginal and demure in white.*)

The End.